Supermarine 1

Books

AVIATION INDUSTRY SERIES, VOLUME 2

Title page image: Supermarine S.6 N247. (*Aeroplane*)

Contents page image: Spitfire F.21s of 615 Squadron.

Published by Key Books
An imprint of Key Publishing Ltd
PO Box 100
Stamford
Lincs PE19 1XQ

www.keypublishing.com

Original edition published as *Aeroplane: Supermarine Company Profile 1913–1960* © 2012, edited by Martyn Chorlton

This edition © 2022

ISBN 978 1 80282 371 4

Typeset by SJmagic DESIGN SERVICES, India.

Contents

The Supermarine Story

The name 'Supermarine' was created by Noel Pemberton Billing back in 1913 who, thankfully for the future of British Aviation, made the wise decision to build 'boats that will fly, and not just aeroplanes with floats!'

The first flying boat designed and built by Pemberton Billing was the P.B.1. The single-engined tractor arrangement aircraft was very pleasing to the eye with its cigar-shaped hull and it made its first public appearance in March 1914.

On the outbreak of war, Pemberton Billing responded to the national requirement for a single-seat fighting scout. The result was the P.B.9, an aircraft that was designed and built in a short period of time, but not as short as implied by its nickname, the 'Seven Day Bus'.

From 1914, Hubert Scott-Paine became the works manager and, from 1916, with Pemberton Billing concentrating on his political career, he became managing director. The same year, the company was renamed The Supermarine Aviation Works Ltd established on the banks of the River Itchen at Woolston, Southampton.

During the First World War, like so many other fledgling aircraft manufacturers, early aircraft orders were sub-contracted from other companies that could not cope, including, in Supermarine's case, Short Brothers machines. The company also carried out experimental work for the Admiralty, including the Push-Proj in 1915, a single-seat pusher scout. The following year, a pair of novel quadruplanc landplanes were also designed to deal with the threat of the Zeppelin. The year 1916 also saw the arrival of the company's most influential aircraft designer, Reginald J. Mitchell, who was partly responsible for the N.1B Baby, Supermarine's most successful design of the First World War.

Above left: Noel Pemberton Billing, one of the most eccentric early British aviators, who was the founding father of Supermarine. (*Aeroplane*)

Above right: The Supermarine works on the River Itchen, at Woolston, Southampton in early 1918. To the left is the Billing yacht basin and, on the right, an A.D. flying boat is prepared for launching. (*Aeroplane*)

Four diverse paths

The company just managed to keep itself going, despite the post war demise of aviation, with a new commercial flying boat called the Channel. A civilianised wartime design, the flying boat could carry three passengers in front of the pilot, and despite only ten being built, they managed to spread themselves from South America to Japan.

It was from this point that the future of Supermarine took four different paths that could be tracked through to the post Second World War era. The first route began with a series of general-purpose single-engine amphibians which began with the Seagull. The genre grew through the 1920s and 1930s and concluded with the Seagull ASR.I amphibian in 1948.

Next were the big twin-engined flying boats, beginning with the highly successful Southampton in 1925 and ending with the Stranraer in 1936. At the same time, a completely different kind of aircraft was being designed for the Schneider Trophy air races, beginning in 1919 and continuing through to 1931. It was this year when, having won the trophy three times in a row, the rules dictated that Britain become the permanent holder of the trophy. The last of the breed of these highly developed seaplane racers, the S.6B, was the world's first aircraft to breach 400mph.

Finally came Supermarine's most significant single event when R J Mitchell began his first designs for Air Ministry Specification F.7/30. Now armed with a wealth of experience and data from the Schneider machines and backed by a highly experienced and efficient technical team, a fighter began to emerge called the Spitfire. First flying on 5 March 1936 in the competent hands of Chief Test Pilot 'Mutt' Summers, the Spitfire, with its beautiful elliptical wing, enclosed cockpit and retractable undercarriage was destined to be one, if not *the*, most successful fighter of World War Two.

Taking the Schneider Trophy

Supermarine's first entry into the 1919 Schneider Trophy contest was the Sea Lion I pusher flying boat. The Sea Lion was damaged on take-off and withdrawn from a race that turned out to be a fiasco, with the only finisher being an Italian who was unfairly disqualified for flying the wrong course. The Italians won the trophy in 1920 and 1921 and were looking set to take the trophy for a third time, which would have prematurely brought the competition to an end. Both the French and Italian entrants were backed, financially, by their respective governments but, typically, Britain was not. This did not stop Supermarine from financing its own entry, the Sea Lion II, which was still based on the six-year-old N.1B Baby designed by R J Mitchell. With test pilot Henri Biard at the controls, the Sea Lion II won the 1922 Schneider Trophy with an average speed of 145.7mph.

The Sea Lion II was also entered for the 1923 event but, despite modifications, Mitchell could only do so much, and the trophy was won by the US with a Curtiss CR.3 twin-float seaplane, a layout that was not overlooked by the staff of Supermarine.

1923 also saw the arrival of the Sea Eagle flying boat with a cabin spacious enough for six passengers. The following year, the Swan appeared, a big amphibian powered by a pair of Rolls-Royce Eagle engines. The Scarab was also produced and supplied to the Spanish Air Force and the range of design ability within the company was demonstrated at the 1924 Lympne Light Aeroplane trials by the two-seat Sparrow.

Breaking technical barriers

The year 1925 saw Supermarine rise to a new technical level, represented by the outstanding Southampton Mk I flying boat. Attractive from every angle, the Napier Lion powered flying boat would serve the RAF until late 1936. In 1926, the Air Ministry decided to make all-metal construction the norm and the first aircraft to be chosen was the Southampton. With its new metal hull, the big flying boat became the Mk II and compared to the older wooden-hulled

The staff of R J Mitchell's drawing office at Woolston in 1923. (Back row, left to right), Arthur Shirvall, Frank Holroyd, George Kettlewell and Joe Smith. (Front row, left to right), Miss Haines, Mr Harris and Miss Attwater. (*Aeroplane*)

machines, which absorbed up to 300lb of water whilst moored, the new aircraft was a sprightlier performer.

The S.4 was introduced in 1925, the first of the racing seaplanes that was way ahead of its time with its un-braced cantilever mid-wing and floats on cantilever struts. Powered by a 700hp Napier Lion, the S.4 managed 226.75mph at Calshot on 13 September 1925. Unfortunately, after a catalogue of problems, the S.4 crashed the day before the 1925 Schneider Trophy at Baltimore was due to be held. The pilot, Biard, was extremely lucky to survive.

It was not until the 1927 Schneider Trophy that the British government finally supported the event and ordered seven high-speed seaplanes. Three of the aircraft were the S.5, which went on to come first and second that year's event at Venice with an average speed of 273.01mph. Before the year was over, an S.5 raised the British speed record to 319.57mph.

Another new flying boat, intended for the Danish Navy, was built in 1928 and called the Nanok. Very similar in design to the Southampton, it was powered by three Armstrong Siddeley Jaguar engines; the aircraft was never delivered to the Danish. It was, however, converted into a luxurious civilian aircraft for the Hon A E Guinness and renamed the Solent.

1928 also saw the Supermarine Aviation Works Ltd swallowed up by the vast Vickers (Aviation) Ltd. The following year, the close co-operation that would last for decades began with the Rolls-Royce/Supermarine partnership. The 1,900hp Rolls-Royce R engine was now available and Mitchell wasted no time, incorporating it into the latest Schneider machines, the S.6s. Not dissimilar to the S.5, but bigger, the S.6 was an outstanding performer, going on to win the 1929 Schneider Trophy with an average speed of 328.63mph. Only days later, the same aircraft raised the world speed record to 357.7mph.

Keeping the Schneider for Britain

Britain was now poised to win the Schneider for a third time as the 1931 event approached, but unbelievably, the government/Air Ministry decided not to finance it. Supermarine could not manage the cost on its own this time, but when Lady Houston offered £100,000, the government yielded to pressure and u-turned in January 1931, leaving Mitchell and his team very little time to prepare. However, in the space of six months, two improved versions of the S.6, the S.6B were built, both fitted with an uprated Rolls-Royce engine capable of producing 2,300hp. The race proved to be an anti-climax as Britain was the only competitor and the event was won in a 'fly-over' at 340.08mph. The S.6B later raised the air speed record again to 407.5mph.

Another busy year was 1931 with the introduction of the Scapa, which came about when a Southampton was fitted with a pair of Rolls Royce Kestrel engines. Two years later, the Seagull name was revived with the Mk V, another private venture. The single-engined amphibian was designed to be catapulted from warships and several were ordered by the Royal Australian Navy. It would go on to become the Walrus in British service and see extensive military service across the globe during World War Two. The Scapa only enjoyed a few years in RAF service before its successor, the Stranraer, was introduced. Originally called the Southampton Mk V, the Stranraer served the RAF into the early war years and the Royal Canadian Navy into the post-war period.

The Spitfire story

In 1934, R J Mitchell designed the Type 224 'Spitfire' in response to the uninspiring Air Ministry Specification F.7/30. The aircraft, a single-seat fighter, was powered by a steam-cooled Goshawk, had a cranked wing and a 'trousered' undercarriage. With a top speed of just 228mph, the aircraft was, unsurprisingly, a failure.

Above left: Reginald Joseph Mitchell poses uncomfortably for the camera. (Via Martyn Chorlton)

Above right: Hubert Scott-Paine, who became General Manager of Pemberton Billing Ltd from 1914 and then took full control of the Supermarine Aviation Works Ltd. (*Aeroplane*)

Not to be deterred, Mitchell began work on a new design project, a machine with lines that had never been seen before. At the same time, another more forward-thinking Air Ministry specification was issued, namely F.5/34, which called for a fighter that could mount eight guns in the wings and would be powered by the 1,000hp Rolls-Royce PV.12 liquid-cooled twelve-cylinder engine, later known as the Merlin. The new specification could not have been better timed, as Supermarine and Hawker were destined to produce two of the country's most significant aircraft: the Spitfire and the Hurricane.

It was around the PV.12 engine that Mitchell began to draw his new fighter, followed by the pilot and then the eight machine guns. While the fuselage retained a hint of Schneider, the wing was of an incredibly advanced design, with a thin aerofoil, low area and an elliptical shape. The Spitfire would become the ultimate fighter pilot's machine, combining great performance and good firepower with a docility that meant that the aircraft was relatively easy to fly. First flown on 5 March 1936 from Eastleigh, the Spitfire had a top speed of 349.5mph, making it the world's fastest military aircraft of the day. Recognising its capabilities, the Air Ministry placed an order for 310 Spitfires on 3 June 1936; many, many more would follow.

Sadly, the Spitfire's creator and the company's Chief Designer from 1919, passed away on 11 June 1937. R J Mitchell CBE had been battling cancer from 1936 and was destined never to see his greatest creation in military service. The design baton was passed to Joseph Smith, who had been working with Vickers-Armstrongs since 1921. Smith always operated in the shadow of his predecessor, but he was the man who saw the Spitfire through many years of development and kept Supermarine at the forefront of aircraft design through the tough post-war years as well.

On 4 August 1938, the Spitfire Mk I, capable of 362mph, joined the RAF with 19 Squadron at Duxford. The same year saw more company changes when Supermarine Aviation Works (Vickers) Ltd and the parent Vickers (Aviation) Ltd of Weybridge were taken over by Vickers-Armstrongs Ltd. While Vickers at Weybridge would go on to concentrate on bomber production, Supermarine became the specialists in fighters and marine aircraft types.

The Second World War

Orders for Spitfires were on the increase by 1939, and a new shadow factory was being built in Castle Bromwich. In the background, a replacement for the Walrus, the Sea Otter, was also being produced but Supermarine's Spitfire commitments meant that all of the amphibian's production was transferred to Saunders-Roe at Cowes on the Isle of Wight.

Meanwhile, the war gained momentum and, at first, the only action seen by Spitfires were occasional hit and run raiders while the Hurricane was being employed over in France. Once that country fell, the Battle of Britain began and both the Spitfire Mk I and Mk II achieved legendary status, along with their young pilots, keeping the Luftwaffe at bay.

The Luftwaffe did manage to hurt Supermarine directly in September 1940 when the Woolston factory was heavily bombed. The company HQ and the design staff were all later moved to the relative safety of Hursley Park, near Winchester, and, by 1944, the entire Supermarine operation was spread across 63 dispersal sites.

By 1941, specialist photographic reconnaissance Spitfires were being built/converted and the Spitfire Mk V was introduced, becoming the backbone of Fighter Command until 1942. The Mk V, which was developed from the private venture Mk III, helped to take the fight back to the enemy with large sweeps over France.

The pressurised Mk VI followed, designed to deal with high-flying German bombers that never materialised. The next Spitfire, Mk VII, had an improved airframe, a two-stage supercharged Merlin 61 and extended wing tips for high-altitude performance. The Mk VIII was an unpressurised version of the Mk VII and the majority saw service in the Middle East.

In response to the Fw 190, one of the most successful and prolific marks of Spitfire came about. The Mk IX had a maximum speed of 402mph and an impressive climb rate and by the end of its production run, over 6,000 had been built. The Mk X and XI and later XIII followed, all of which were photographic variants, while the 2,000hp Griffon-powered Mk XII was introduced with low flying Fw 190 fighter bombers. The Mk XIV, with a top speed of 429mph, proved useful during Operation *Overlord* and tackling V-1 flying bombs. The Mk XVI introduced the Packard Merlin 266 while the XVIII was built with stronger wings and more fuel capacity. The Mk XIX, despite appearing late in the war, was based on the Mk XIV and was a dedicated photographic reconnaissance machine. A single Mk XX was also built with the excellent Griffon IIB engine but, by this stage, the aircraft proved more useful in the development of the final Spitfire variants, the F.21, 22 and 24.

The last Spitfires were powered by the Griffon 61, 64 or 85 engine and all three, the F.21, 22 and F.24 had a completely redesigned stronger wing and a maximum speed of around 450mph. Only the F.21 saw some brief service during the tail end of the war, but all went on to serve the RAF in the early 1950s, the majority with Royal Auxiliary Air Force squadrons.

Below left: **The Woolston factory pictured during the late 1920s with only a single Southampton hull visible. (***Aeroplane***)**

Below right: **The huge Supermarine drawing office at Woolston in 1938. Following some unwanted attention from the Luftwaffe in late 1940, the office was moved to Hursley Park, near Winchester. The large stately home was requisitioned from Sir George Cooper of Strong's Breweries. (***Aeroplane***)**

From the prototype first flying, through to the arrival of the F.22 in 1945, the top speed of the Spitfire had been raised by 100mph and the climb rate had been doubled. By the end of production, 20,351 Spitfires had been built.

The Seafire

The Royal Navy had to wait an agonising amount of time before it received its own navalised Spitfire, which would become the Seafire. Throughout its service career with the Royal Navy, the type had struggled and it was not until the final variant, the Seafire F.47, that the aircraft finally found its sea legs, albeit a little late in the day. The Seafire Mk III was the World War Two workhorse serving in many theatres from the Mediterranean to the Kamikaze finale over the Pacific in 1945. 2,408 Seafires were built as Mk I, II, III, XV, XVII, F.45, F.46 and F.47, the latter being retired from FAA service 1950.

Post-war

As World War Two drew to a close, the reality of having to design a replacement for the Spitfire began to dawn. The new fighter would have to be fast and the only way to improve the top speed was to improve the wing. The new 'Spitfire' was the Spiteful, which was fitted with a straight-tapered laminar flow wing but still powered by a Rolls-Royce Griffon. The Spiteful would never see action but, in 1947, the prototype reached a top speed of 494mph, making it the second fastest piston-engined aircraft in the world.

However, the Spiteful was set to be a distant memory with the arrival of the jet-powered Attacker, which was first flown by Jeffrey Quill in July 1946. With a maximum speed of 590mph, the Attacker was propelled by a Rolls-Royce Nene and first entered FAA service in August 1951. Prior to this, test pilot Mike Lithgow broke the world record for a 100km closed-circuit at a speed of 564.881mph.

Despite the lack of military orders from its own country that always follows a conflict, Supermarine continued to sell the Spitfire overseas, and a few trainer conversions were also produced and several Sea Otters were converted for civilian use as well. The company had not quite finished producing marine types either, and, in 1948, the latest version of the Seagull, the ASR.I was shown to the public for the first time. The very neat-looking design the aircraft incorporated a variable-incidence high-lift wing, which the company had developed with the Type 322 'Dumbo' during the early war years. The wing gave the Seagull a speed range of 54 to 260mph but despite its excellent qualities, the Air Ministry were now turning to long range land-based aircraft to carry out the same role.

The Cold War jets

The Attacker featured in the company's second jet design the Type 510 high-speed research aircraft. First flown on 28 December 1948, the Type 510 had the fuselage of an Attacker with swept wings and, when it was fitted with an 'A' frame arrester hook, it became the first swept wing jet fighter to land and take off from an aircraft carrier; once again in the hands of Mike Lithgow.

The Type 528 followed, now with an afterburner and, once fitted with a nose wheel undercarriage, was designated the Type 535, which first appeared at the SBAC in 1950. There was only one more stage to the Type 541, by now known as the Swift, which went on to be powered by the Rolls-Royce Avon.

Alan N Clifton, the head of the Supermarine technical office from the early 1920s and the chief designer following Joe Smith. (*Aeroplane*)

Above left: The Attacker prototype TS409 with Mike Lithgow at the controls, prior to being delivered to the A&AEE at Boscombe Down. (*Aeroplane*)

Above right: VV119, the Type 535, which was first flown by Mike Lithgow from Boscombe Down on 23 August 1950. This beautiful jet is pictured with Supermarine test pilot Dave Morgan at the controls. (*Aeroplane*)

The story of the Swift is a troubled one, which saw early marks grounded for safety reasons and later marks cancelled by the hundred as the RAF steered towards the Hawker Hunter. While the Swift F.1 and F.2 saw very brief service, it was only the photographic variant, the FR.5, that saw any significant service. One highlight of the aircraft's career occurred on 5 July 1953, when Mike Lithgow, in a Swift F.4, broke the London to Paris speed record, averaging 669.3mph. On 25 September 1953, with Lithgow at the controls again, a new world air speed record was achieved at 737.3mph.

The final and most technically challenging aircraft to be designed and solely produced by Supermarine was the Scimitar. The Scimitar story was a protracted one which began with the Type 505, 508, 529 and 535. The Type 508 made its maiden flight from Boscombe Down on 31 August 1951. The result of these development aircraft was the Type 544 Scimitar which entered FAA service in 1958. The Scimitar was an engineering marvel, which pioneered new methods of airframe construction including the use of titanium components and the introduction of chemical etching to remove surplus metal from surface skins. The Scimitar enjoyed an awkward service career with the FAA until its retirement in 1968 with a high loss rate and equally high maintenance per flying rate as well. The knowledge gained from the Scimitar's development and construction would prove invaluable for the TSR.2 and much later with the Tornado that still serves the RAF today.

In 1960, following yet another reorganisation of the country's aircraft manufacturing, BAC (British Aircraft Corporation) was born. As a result, four major companies were absorbed to form BAC, English Electric, Bristol, Hunting and Vickers-Armstrongs (Aircraft). This was a merger too far for Supermarine, and the name was sadly lost within the Vickers-Armstrongs, which was absorbed, along with Hawker Siddeley and Scottish Aviation to form British Aerospace in 1977. Today, following the latest reorganisation in 1999, it is known as BAE Systems.

Below left: The Swift FR.5 was an aircraft that spent most of its short career at low-level. This 2 Squadron machine is captured at altitude during its service from Geilenkirchen and later Jever, both in West Germany, from February 1956 to March 1961. (*Aeroplane*)

Below right: The first of three production aircraft designated N.113D and built as a Type 544 Scimitar was WT854. The big jet pictured on HMS *Ark Royal* during proving trials in January 1957. (Via Martyn Chorlton)

Pemberton Billing

P.B. Glider (Revised P.B.0)

Noel Pemberton Billing's interest in aviation began in about 1903 and, like so many pioneers of the day, his thoughts turned to gliders. His first creation, the Pemberton-Billing Glider, later referred to as the P.B.0, was a classic homemade affair. However, it was a novel triangular kite design, which broke the mould slightly, although its first flight from the roof of his house in East Grinstead in 1904 nearly brought the young man's life to an abrupt end.

Right: **Pemberton Billing's first attempt at flight using a triangular kite show during his leap of faith from the roof of his house. (Martyn Chorlton)**

Below: **The P.B.1 at the Olympia Aero Show in 1914. (Martyn Chorlton)**

The NEC-powered P.B.5 was never flown and was sold off to clear Pemberton-Billing's debts. (Martyn Chorlton)

P.B. Monoplanes

Undeterred by his earlier experience, Pemberton Billing's next aircraft was a small monoplane, later referred to as the P.B.1. The pusher design was powered by a valveless rotary engine and had a tubular chassis with a tricycle undercarriage. Once again, though, the aircraft refused to fly when tested at Woolston in 1909.

The second Pemberton Billing Monoplane, later known as the P.B.3, was a modified version of the P.B.1. Changes included extending the wings aft at the root, which ended in a flap arrangement from which lateral and directional control could be achieved. Powered by a two-cylinder JAP engine, the P.B.3 showed more promise and, during early flight testing, the monoplane showed a willingness to leave the ground. Unfortunately, the P.B.3's most successful flight, to a height of almost 60ft, resulted in a crash, injuring Pemberton Billing.

This period of monoplane designs ended with the third in the series, which became the P.B.5. Very similar to the P.B.3, the latest monoplane had the potential for more control thanks to the fitment of a front elevator. Powered by a more purposeful NEC four-cylinder engine, the P.B.5 was never flown and was sold to help clear Pemberton Billings, debts while he recovered from the injuries incurred in the P.B.3 crash.

It was during 1909 that Pemberton Billing also became involved in an ambitious project to establish a large aerodrome and aircraft factory at South Fambridge, Essex. Influential aviation pioneers of the day were attracted to the project, including Howard Wright and Weis and McFie, but the project was sadly doomed to failure. The remote location, marshy terrain, not to mention a large ditch straddling the take-off area, saw the idea dissolve with a year.

P.B.1 (Revised P.B.7)

Pemberton Billing Ltd was not registered as a company until 27 June 1914, but this did not stop the eccentric from producing his first flying boat design, which was on display at the Olympia Aero Show in 1914. The aircraft was a very attractive, petite single-seat flying boat called the Supermarine P.B.1. Pemberton Billing had been building fast launches at a site near to the Woolston Ferry on the River Itchen, Southampton, since 1912 and he was consumed with the idea of flying above the waves rather than ploughing through them. Pemberton Billing adopted the name Supermarine for his telegraphic address and it was this name that featured so prominently as a prefix for future aircraft, despite the company being known as Vickers-Supermarine from 1928.

The P.B.1 had a hull shaped like a fish, complete with flared sponsons and bottom planes integrated with the upper frames of the hull. The attractive design was the work of marine architect Linton Hope;

a man who introduced yacht production techniques into flying boat hulls. The pilot was positioned behind the biplane wings and the engine was mounted in front of the wings above the nose at a high thrust angle driving a three-blade propeller. The unequal span wings were constructed as one section without any dihedral and sprung, circular section floats were mounted under the outboard interplane struts. While control surfaces were conventional, novel features included a 'Supermeter' for measuring height above the water on landing and a Grapnel was fitted in the nose as well.

The high thrust angle of the engine and lack of power from the alleged 50hp Gnome were contributory factors to the P.B.1 not being able to take off. Unperturbed, Pemberton Billing and Linton Hope redesigned the P.B.1 by swapping the positions of the pilot and engine. The engine was now buried in the hull driving two pusher propellers via chain drives. Despite the effort to improve the P.B.1 (Modified), it still refused fly when tested by Howard Pixton again in May 1914. Less than year later, the company's first aircraft was broken up at Woolston.

Monoplane flying boat

The P.B.2 had a similar hull-design to the P.B.1, although the lower hull portion extended much further aft. Power was to be provided by a 120hp Austro-Daimler engine fitted into the hull driving a 9ft diameter three-bladed PB Trinity propeller in a tractor configuration. The pilot sat in a rear cockpit, but the larger fuselage allowed for a second cockpit, under the wing, which could have been large enough for two passengers.

The monoplane wing was mounted above the fuselage on struts and was braced by thin chord aerofoils. The under floats were similar to those fitted to the P.B.1 and were also sprung via an effective system of struts.

Once again though, the thrust-line of the propeller shaft was at a steep angle and potential flight could have been a struggle. Regardless, the P.B.2 never left the drawing board.

P.B.3

A larger version of the P.B.2 that was also never built, the P.B.3 was intended to be the first of Pemberton-Billings' 'slip-wing' designs. The 'slip-wing' idea was that an aircraft suffered an engine failure, after landing in the sea, the wings could be shed and the aircraft could continue on its way using an auxiliary marine engine. The aircraft was also described as having an 'alternative drive', which was most likely one way of saying the 'craft' had a submersible propeller as per a normal marine craft.

The larger scale of the P.B.3 warranted two 90hp Austro-Daimler engines powering a pair of 9ft 6in diameter three-bladed PB Trinity propellers. The aircraft was also to have using wing warping for lateral control but, like its predecessor, was never built.

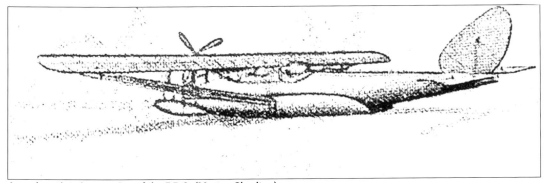

A crude artists impression of the P.B.2. (Martyn Chorlton)

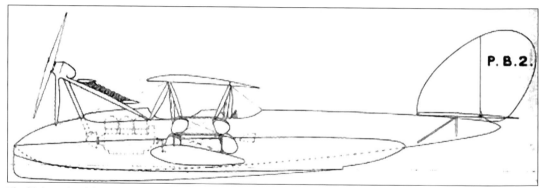

The high angle of the propeller shaft of the P.B.2 is evident in this line drawing. (Martyn Chorlton)

P.B.5 (Revised P.B.21) and P.B.7 (Revised P.B.19)

During 1914, Pemberton Billing managed to secure an order for twelve Short S.38 dual-control from the Admiralty. Rather than resting on his laurels and preparing for a period of building other manufacturers during the forthcoming world war, he continued to work on his own designs.

Continuing the 'slip-wing' thinking, the next project was the P.B.5 later redesignated as the P.B.21. The P.B.5 never left the drawing board but the P.B.7 later known as the P.B.19. Two P.B.7s were actually ordered by the German Navy in April 1914 and construction commenced the following month.

The P.B.7 was a large biplane with a pair of Salmson or Sunbeam engines mounted within the hull driving a pair of pusher propellers using chain-drive. The hull was basically a motor boat, complete with standard marine propeller and a rudder. The rear part of fuselage, complete with tail surfaces and the entire wing unit were attached as one piece and could be detached accordingly.

By July 1914, one of the P.B.7s was nearing completion but world events took over and all further work on both aircraft was abandoned when the First World War broke out.

At least one of the motor boat sections of a P.B.7 was used later on the Solent.

P.B.9 (revised P.B.13)

Pemberton Billing's next aircraft was a private venture that became known as the 'Seven Day Bus', or the P.B.9 later revised to P.B.13. Built in August 1914 on the verge of the outbreak of the First World War, Pemberton Billing was at loggerheads with War Office's aviation policy at the time, and he made a great deal of effort to promote how quickly and easily a fighting scout could be produced. However, the aircraft may have been constructed in seven days (from 3 to 11 August 1914) but Pemberton Billing certainly had a head-start.

Firstly, Pemberton Billing claimed he designed the aircraft himself, based on some sketches he drew on the factory walls. In fact, the P.B.9 was designed by Carol Vasilesco. It is also known that Pemberton Billing purchased a large amount of components from the Radley-England Enterprise company including a set of wings, intended for use in a small pusher 'water-plane'. It was then a straightforward

Traces of the P.B.7 would reappear in post-war flying boat designs. (Martyn Chorlton)

Artist's impression of the P.B.11 which displayed all the signs of being a Farman III. (Martyn Chorlton)

process of designing a fuselage and tail unit to mate up with the Radley-England wings. The fuselage was a simply braced mortise and tenon construction, which could have produced by any good standard joiner's shop. It was Pemberton Billing's idea to encourage massed and quick production by involving furniture manufacture's in the building of aircraft.

On 12 August 1914, the P.B.9 was taken to a field near Netley, Hampshire, and, in the hands of Sopwith test pilot Victor Mahl, took to the air for the first time. It was said to have performed well but no order for the scout type biplane was forthcoming.

Pemberton Billing did not take the disinterest in his latest endeavour well and he began to distance himself from his own company to carry out some service with the naval air arm. Woolston was now in the hands of Hubert Scott-Paine, who, over time, began to be a much more prominent figure within the business than Pemberton-Billing. Scott-Paine also won over the Air Department and Admiralty while Pemberton Billing concentrated on his political career and ambitions.

Later transferred to Brooklands, the P.B.9 was then passed to the RNAS and, by 1915, was displaying the serial No.1267 at Chingford and Hendon. SOC (Struck off Charge) by late 1915, Pemberton Billing acquired the P.B.9 to help promote his failed bid to become elected as an MP for East Hertfordshire in March 1916. By now, Pemberton-Billing had moved on from the aviation industry and his company was renamed as the Supermarine Aviation Works Ltd.

P.B.11 (Revised P.B.15)

It is most likely that the P.B.11 was no more than a Farman III powered by Gnome rotary engine. It is believed that this was the aircraft that Pemberton Billing bought in 1913, so he could win a bet with Frederick Handley Page. Handley Page wagered that Pemberton Billing could not learn to fly in 24 hours. However, Pemberton Billing began his 'crash' course at 0545hrs on the morning of 17 September at the Vickers School of Flying, Brooklands and by breakfast had won the £500 bet! However, photographic evidence shows Pemberton Billing under instruction from Harold Barnwell at Brooklands in a Bristol Boxkite?

Serialled No.1374, the aircraft went on to serve with RNAS from February 1915.

P.B.13 (Revised P.B.17)

The P.B.13 was a proposed larger version of the P.B.9 with staggered wings but still by a Gnome rotary. Redesignated as the P.B.17, the final Pemberton Billing scout design was never built.

P.B.23E 'Push-Proj'

Most likely inspired by Harold Bolas of the Air Department and the Admiralty under Murray Sueter, who Pemberton Billing was close to at the time, the P.B.23E was a simple, low-drag design.

Above left: A tricky little fighter to fly, only one P.B.23 'Push-Proj' was built and it is pictured here at Hendon during its flight trials in September 1915. (Martyn Chorlton)

Above right: The P.B.9 was probably the most successful aircraft produced by Pemberton Billing in the shortest space of time. (Martyn Chorlton)

Left: The second P.B.25 to be built was No.9001, which shows the sweepback to adjust the centre of gravity to good effect in this view. (Martyn Chorlton)

Flight trials of the prototype began at Hendon in September 1915, but the slippery little fighter suffered from instability, mainly caused by the centre of gravity being too far to the rear. Straight-line performance was excellent and P.B.23E was one of the fastest biplanes of the day. The centre of gravity issue was solved by sweeping back the wings and the redesign resulted in the P.B.25.

The name 'Push-Proj' is short for 'pushed projectile', and the pleasing shape of the fuselage also earned the P.B.23E the nickname 'Sparklet' because the nacelle looked like a Sparklet bulb.

P.B.25 'Scout' (1916)

The P.B.25 came about in early 1916 because of the modifications made to the P.B.23E which was mainly the introduction of an 11° sweepback of both wings and inversely tapered ailerons. The other significant change was that the nacelle was fabric-covered, replacing the metal-covered version of the P.B.23E.

Despite the changes, the P.B.25 still exuded poor handling qualities and the delicate structure of the nacelle did not give pilots any confidence in the event of a nose-over on landing. Of the 20 P.B.25s built, none were used operationally although several were flown at Eastchurch, the Isle of Grain and Killingholme. The last was delivered to the RNAS in February 1917.

At a time when fighting scouts were desperately needed, the P.B.25 should have been in the frame for a large order. However, a shortage of engine and a lack of time for development saw other types quickly supersede the P.B.25.

A later view about the intended use for the P.B.25 suggested that Pemberton Billing wanted the aircraft as a short-range escort for the anti-airship P.B.29E and P.B.31E quadruplanes.

P.B.29E

During 1915, the Zeppelin, however ineffective we view it today, was posing a serious threat to Britain's morale and any effort to oppose it was fully supported by the government. Aircraft manufacturers were

Above left: The only P.B.29E 'Zeppelin Destroyer' built, which first flew briefly in the autumn of 1915. (Martyn Chorlton)

Above right: P.B.31E No.1388 proudly displaying the new formed Supermarine Aviation Works Ltd, Southampton logo along its rear fuselage. The aircraft marked the last of an interesting line of Pemberton Billing machines. (Martyn Chorlton)

actively encouraged to design and construct aircraft capable of attacking Zeppelins and Pemberton Billing's offering was the P.B.29E.

The P.B.29E was a twin-engined high aspect ratio quadruplane, which was designed to operate at low speed at night. Powered by a pair of 90hp Austro-Daimler engines which were under-slung from the second mainplane, the aircraft had a crew of two. The pilot was positioned in a rear cockpit in the fuselage while the air gunner was in a front cockpit. A nacelle was also located between the centre sections of the upper mainplanes for the air gunner to climb into during the flight.

Very crude in appearance, the P.B.29E is believed to have first flown in autumn 1915, but its flying career was short lived and the novel aircraft was wrecked not long after.

P.B.31E NightHawk

The P.B.31E was an improved version of the P.B.29E, which was the first aircraft to be known as a Supermarine type. In December 1916, Pemberton Billing Ltd changed its name to Supermarine Aviation Works Ltd (under the control of Hubert Scott-Paine), and by this time the P.B.31E was unofficially known as the Supermarine 'NightHawk'.

Once again a quadruplane, the P.B.31E first flew in February 1917 and on the face of it was no more than a scaled up and slightly more comfortable version of the P.B.29E. It was designed to have a ground-breaking endurance of 18 hours, in theory giving the aircraft the ability to lie in wait for an approaching Zeppelin. Armament was beefed up with a Davis non-recoil gun, able to fire a 1½lb shell and a Scarff ring mounted Lewis .303in machine gun, both mounted in the centre of the upper wing. An additional .303in Lewis machine gun could also be mounted on a Scarff ring in the nose, forward of the fully enclosed cockpit. Another unique feature was the provision for a gimbal-mounted searchlight in the nose which was powered by a 5hp ABC flat-twin engine and generator.

The P.B.31E performed very well during flight testing at Eastbourne in the hands of Clifford B Prodger although the twin 100hp Anzani engines did not give enough power to an aircraft of this size. Prodger only managed a top speed of 75mph, although the required low landing speed for night operations was an acceptable 35mph.

In theory, the lumbering PB.31E would have stood little chance of catching Zeppelin let alone shooting it down, and on 23 July 1917, the one and only prototype, No.1388 was scrapped and the concept was abandoned.

A.D. (Air Department) Flying-Boat

Development

After Pemberton-Billing departed to focus on his political career, Hubert Scott-Paine now concentrated on working directly with the Admiralty. Contracts for the construction Type 184s, P.B.25s and the Nighthawk were coming to an end and more work of a more progressive nature was needed if the fledgling Supermarine Aviation Works was to survive.

History

The overall Supermarine design was carried out by Harris Booth, although Linton Hope is credited with the lines and structure of the hull, which would give the A.D. Flying boat flexibility when dealing with rough or choppy seas. The A.D. was a biplane of conventional configuration and the tail and rudders were also a biplane design. Pilot and observer sat in tandem cockpits in the nose while the engine was located above and behind them below the upper mainplane. To aid ship-board stowage, the wings could also be folded.

Two prototypes were built, No.1412 and 1413, the first of which was planned to be powered by 150 Sunbeam Nubian, but this was replaced by a Hispano-Suiza 8 because of production delays. The aircraft was a bit of handful at first, especially during take-off when the A.D. porpoised itself uncomfortably into the air. After several modifications, including revisions to the hull, fin and rudders a production order was placed.

Operational service

The first production aircraft, N1290, completed its acceptance trials at the Isle of Grain on 5 September 1917. The majority of the 27 aircraft built were placed into store but N1712 and N1719 were sent to the Isle of Grain NAS (Naval Air Station) served in an experimental role. N1719 was later fitted with hydrovanes and flown by Harry Busteed and Bentley Dacre in this configuration.

Nineteen of the A.D. Flying Boats built were purchased by Supermarine after the end of the First World War and converted in Channel Mk Is and Mk IIs.

Production

The two prototypes, No.1412 and 1413, were built under CP 109611/5 while the official first batch was N1290-1299 (10), of which only N1290 was built by J. Samuel White and Company under AS.14609. The first production run of just ten aircraft was N1520-1529 built by Supermarine under AS.5288/17. Three of this batch were later converted to Channel Mk Is while N1525 was used for trials with the Wolseley Python and Viper engines.

The third production batch of another ten aircraft was N1710-1719 ordered under AS.20798. Half of these went on to become Channels. The final ambitious order for 50 aircraft, N2450-2499 was ordered under AS.18936. However, only six aircraft, N2450-2455, were built and two of these were later converted to Channels. Total production was 27 aircraft.

Technical data – A.D. Flying-Boat	
ENGINE	One 200hp Hispano-Suiza
WINGSPAN	50ft 4in
WINGSPAN (Folded)	14ft
LENGTH	30ft 7in
LENGTH (Folded)	42ft 3in
HEIGHT	13ft 1in
WING AREA	455 sq ft
EMPTY WEIGHT	2,508lb
LOADED WEIGHT	3,567lb
MAX SPEED	100mph
ALIGHTING SPEED	46mph
ENDURANCE	4½hrs
ARMAMENT	One .303in Lewis machine-gun in bow cockpit

The prototype A.D. Boat No.1412, the first of 27 built. (Via _Aeroplane_)

The A.D.1 Navyplane

Development

As deputy to Harris Booth, the chief designer at the Admiralty's Air Department, Harold Bolas saw himself having to restrain the often 'grotesque' designs that his boss was submitting. However, Booth's strength was his influence on the Board of Admiralty, which saw the introduction of the O/100, 1½ Strutter, Pup and Camel.

The design of a new reconnaissance/bombing seaplane, later designated as the A.D.1, was initiated by Bolas. It was planned that the aircraft would be built in the Air Department's new Experimental Construction Depot at Port Victoria on the Isle of Grain. However, this was still being built and the A.D.1 was passed on to Supermarine at Woolston.

History

A sturdy, compact two-bay biplane, the A.D.1 could carry a two-man crew inside a streamlined monocoque nacelle positioned between the wings. The pilot occupied the rear cockpit while the observer sat in the front or bow position. Power was provided by an air-cooled 150hp Smith Static radial fitted with a four-blade pusher propeller. The A.D.1 sat on twin pontoon floats braced to the nacelle while the twin fins and rudders were fitted between two pairs of tubular steel tail booms.

Operational service

Two prototypes were ordered, No.9095 and No.9096, although only the former was ever completed. The aircraft was ready for flight testing in August 1916 and first flew in the hands of Cdr John Seddon. Little is known about the aircraft's early flight testing and nothing more was heard of the A.D.1 until May 1917. It was now powered by an A.R.I engine, designed by W.O. Bentley, which gave the A.D.1 a much-improved performance but it was still below the requirements called for by the Admiralty.

Production

As well as the order for two prototype A.D.1s, a small production batch of five aircraft, N1070-1074, was placed by the Admiralty with 140hp Smith engines. All were cancelled as it was realised that the A.D.1 Navyplane could not reach the hoped for standard.

Technical data – A.D.1 Navyplane	
ENGINE	One A.R.1 rotary
WINGSPAN	36ft
LENGTH	27ft 9in
HEIGHT	12ft 9in
WING AREA	360 sq ft
EMPTY WEIGHT	2,100lb
LOADED WEIGHT	3,102lb
MAX SPEED	75mph
ALIGHTING SPEED	36mph
ENDURANCE	6hrs
ARMAMENT	One .303in Lewis machine-gun and a single torpedo

The first prototype A.D.1 Navyplane No.9095, with Hubert Scott-Paine (right) and a member of the Admiralty. (*Aeroplane*)

N.1B Baby

Development

The RNAS were very keen to expand the development of single-seat fighters and much time and effort was already being spent at Eastchurch and the Isle of Grain improving the Sopwith Baby. A new specification was issued by the Air Department for a flying boat fighter or single-seat seaplane under specification N.1B. Details included an aircraft that could reach 95 kt (109.5mph) at 10,000ft and the capability to reach 20,000ft. A tall order considering the array of unreliable engines available at the time, but this did not stop Blackburn, Norman Thompson and Supermarine entering designs, all of which were flying boats.

History

Supermarine's N.1B Baby was designed by F J Hargreaves but was clearly influenced by Bolas and his assistant R J Mitchell. The Baby was a single-bay biplane powered by a geared Hispano engine driving a pusher propeller. The hull was a Linton Hope design, similar to the A.D. Boat construction, with a T-tail mounted on top of a single fin. Ailerons were initially fitted to the upper main wing but these were later also attached to the lower one as well.

Operational service

First flown in February 1918, the first of three aircraft, N59, made its maiden flight and, by August 1918, was recording some impressive performance figures. Only N59 was ever finished, but this laid the foundation blocks for the Sea King and the Schneider Sea Lions. The second aircraft, N60 was designed quite differently from the original and was to be powered by a 200hp Sunbeam Arab engine. The third Baby, N61, was laid down by the N.1B specification but was cancelled before it was completed.

Production

Only the three N.1Bs were ordered under contract AS.3929. Only N59 flew, N60 was partially completed and is believed to have still been delivered to Grain as a spare airframe. N61 was partially completed and the hull was possibly used for Sea Lion I.

Technical data – N.1B Baby	
ENGINE	One 200hp Hispano-Suiza and later a 200hp Sunbeam Arab
WINGSPAN	30ft 6in
LENGTH	26ft 4in
HEIGHT	10ft 7in
WING AREA	309 sq ft
EMPTY WEIGHT	1,699lb
LOADED WEIGHT	2,326lb
MAX SPEED (Hispano-Suiza)	117mph at sea level (Arab) 115mph at 10,000ft
ALIGHTING SPEED	57mph
ENDURANCE	3hrs

The sole N.1B Baby, N59, pictured at Grain with its wings folded for shipboard stowage. (Via Martyn Chorlton)

Channel I & II

Development

By 1919, there was a great surplus of military aircraft, many of which, including Supermarine's own A.D. flying boat, were suitable for conversion to passenger-carrying machines. The A.D. would be ideal for flying short-haul sea routes and, by May 1919, Supermarine had purchased ten of them from the Admiralty for conversion into the Channel.

It was hoped that the aircraft could be made ready for flying trips at Whitsun, operating between Southampton, Ryde, Sandown, Shanklin and Ventnor. The plan was that five of the Channels would fly the services, while the remaining five would be used alternately allowing ample time for servicing and inspections.

Design

Conversion from the military A.D. to the civilian Channel Mk I was fairly straightforward. Firstly, one extra cockpit was opened up forward of the mainplanes and the original Hispano-Suiza engine was replaced by a 160hp Beardmore. A small rudder was also added to help to improve the handling of the Channel while taxying.

The additional cockpit allowed the Channel to be used as a three-seat training aircraft or, with further modification, created room for four-passengers. The passenger version was generally used for the pleasure flights and service.

The Channel Mk II differed from the Mk I by being fitted with a 240hp Armstrong Siddeley Puma engine. The Puma engine had been looked at in detail by Supermarine since early 1920 to help improve the take-off performance of the Channel. By October 1920, drawings had been raised and conversion kits were supplied by Supermarine to operators for an upgrade from a Mk I to a Mk II.

Service

The same day the Channel's CofA was issued, on 23 July 1919, the first three aircraft, G-EAED, G-EAEE and G-EAEK began a passenger carrying service from Southampton to Bournemouth. Only a week later, a 72 year old woman and 75 year old man were taken for a pleasure flight in one of the Channels. The same week, several flights were made from Southampton to Cowes with passengers on board who had missed a ferry.

The tasking of the Channels held no bounds and during the national rail strike in 1919, the flying boats delivered thousands of copies of the *Southern Daily Echo* from Southampton to Bournemouth. The papers were received at 0600hrs and by 0643hrs were being rowed ashore at Bournemouth. From September 1919, Channels were also flying across the Channel to Le Havre.

In May 1920, three Channel Mk Is were bought by the Norwegian Airline, Det Norske Luftartrederi, followed by four more in July for the Norwegian Navy, although one crashed on 12 July at Kristiania.

Production/conversions

Ten ex-military A.D. boats were converted by Supermarine to Channel Mk Is, the majority of which were later converted to Mk IIs. Of this batch, two were later delivered to Bermuda and four were later delivered to Norway. An additional four Channels were delivered to the Norwegian Navy, one to the Swedish Navy, one to New Zealand, one to Venezuela/British Guiana, one to Japan and one aircraft to Chile.

Technical data – Channel Mk I And Mk II	
ENGINE	(I) One 160hp Beardmore. (II) One 240hp Armstrong Siddeley Puma
WINGSPAN (Upper)	50ft 5in
WINGSPAN (Lower)	39ft 7in
LENGTH	30ft
HEIGHT	13ft
WING AREA	453 sq ft
EMPTY WEIGHT	2,356lb
LOADED WEIGHT	3,400lb
MAX SPEED	(Mk I) 80mph, (Mk II) 92mph
ALIGHTING SPEED	53mph
CLIMB	3,000ft in 15 min
ENDURANCE	3hrs

The last Channel built was this Mk II for Chile in 1922. It was delivered to the Chilean Naval Air Service as a three-seat armed reconnaissance flying boat and its hull was different from the early Channels and more resembled that of a Seal or Seagull type machine. (Via Martyn Chorlton)

Sea Lion I, Mk II & Mk III

Development

The Schneider Trophy, despite only having been organised on two occasions in 1913 and 1914, was already developing into an event that was nurturing rapid development in marine aviation. Disrupted by the First World War, Supermarine's first opportunity came in 1919 and the company's entry was a development of the N.1B Baby, designed by F J Hargreaves.

Design

The first of three Schneider trophy entries under the name Sea Lion was the Mk I, which took its name from its engine, the Napier Lion. The 450hp unit replaced the Hispanos of the Baby and it is believed that the partially completed hull of N61 help to create Sea Lion Mk I G-EALP. The wings were redesigned with an unequal span and the engine was mounted on its own pylon. The tail looked like the Baby's, although the fin and rudder was scaled up while control surfaces had streamlined aerodynamic balances.

The Sea Lion Mk II, designed by R J Mitchell, was originally built as the Sea King amphibian in 1921 but was rebuilt with a 450hp Napier Lion II engine for the 1922 Schneider Trophy. The Sea King's mainplanes were retained but reduced in area by decreasing the chord. As with the Mk I, the Mk II had an increased fin area and in this case a larger tailplane to compensate for the high torque of the Lion II engine.

The Sea Lion Mk III came about because of the low standard of British entrants for the 1923 Schneider Trophy. Scott-Paine felt obliged to enter another Supermarine aircraft but was reluctant to invest another £6,000 as he had with the Sea Lion Mk II. With little time at hand, it was decided to re-engine and redesign the Mk II so that it could achieve at least 15mph more than the 1922 winner. A 525hp Lion III was fitted and Mitchell increased the wing area, changed the lines of the hull and modified the wingtip floats. To cover costs, the aircraft was purchased by the Air Ministry.

Service

Flown by Sqn Ldr B D Hobbs, Sea Lion Mk I G-EALP was entered into the 1919 Schneider race organised by the Royal Aero Club at Bournemouth. Fog disrupted the race, forcing Hobbs to land in Swanage Bay to get his bearings. Just as the Sea Lion was at the point of taking off, the aircraft struck an object in the water, which punched a hole in the hull. After landing again near Bournemouth pier the flying boat sank.

Sea Lion Mk II G-EBAH was flown by Henri Biard for the 1922 race at Naples and, after flying at an average speed of 145.7mph, won the trophy for Britain. The Sea Lion Mk III, also registered as G-EBAH, was an outsider for the 1923 trophy race but, against the odds, Biard managed to achieve third place having managed an average speed of 157.17mph.

Given the serial N170, the Mk III was delivered to the Air Ministry but, during a flight test, Fg Off E E Paull-Smith crashed off Felixstowe.

Production

Only three aircraft were produced, a single example each of a Mk I, Mk II and a Mk III. Mk I G-EALP was a modified N.1B Bay; Mk II G-EBAH was a converted Sea King II, and the Mk III was the Mk II purchased by the Air Ministry under contract 409868/23 (8 March 1923) and re-serialled N170 but also carried G-EBAH.

Technical data – Sea Lion Mk I, Mk II and Mk III	
ENGINE	(I) One 450hp Napier Lion IA. (II) One 450hp Napier Lion II. (III) One 525hp Napier Lion III
WINGSPAN	(I upper) 35ft (II) 32ft (III) 28ft
LENGTH	(I) 26ft 4in (II) 24ft 9in (III) 28ft
WING AREA	(I) 380 sq ft (II) 384 sq ft (III) 360 sq ft
EMPTY WEIGHT	(I) 2,000lb (II) 2,115lb (III) 2,400lb
LOADED WEIGHT	(I) 2,900lb (II minus undercarriage) 2,850lb (III) 3,275lb
MAX SPEED	(I) 147mph (II) 160mph (III) 175mph
ENDURANCE	(I) 2½hr (II & III) 3hrs

The Supermarine Sea Lion Mk III N-170 after delivery to the Air Ministry on 10 March 1926. (Via Martyn Chorlton)

Commercial Amphibian

Development

It was in April 1920 that the Air Ministry announced a competition to find, 'the best type of Float Seaplanes or Boat Seaplanes which will be safe, comfortable and economical for air travel and capable of alighting on and rising from land as well as water.' The requirements went on and those manufacturers taking part had little time as the competition was planned to begin at Martlesham Heath and Felixstowe on 1 September.

Design

The Commercial Amphibian was a single-engined biplane flying boat with a wooden hull based on the A.D. boat and the Channel. The 350hp Rolls-Royce Eagle VIII engine was positioned between the mainplanes in a pusher configuration.

The hull was a Linton Hope pattern, double skinned in mahogany and covered in doped fabric and finished off with boat-builders' varnish and polish. The non-folding wings were of unequal span with outwardly raked struts. The wings were non-folding so they could accommodate the undercarriage, which was made up of a pair of steel tube frameworks. The Commercial even had a rotatable tailskid, which doubled as a water rudder and the pilot even had a tiller to help him taxy the flying boat on busy waters.

The open cockpit was located in front of the lower mainplane while the passengers were accommodated in an enclosed forward cabin.

Service

It is presumed that the Commercial Amphibian first flew in August 1920, in time to become one of five competitors registered to take part in the Air Ministry competition. In the end, only three made it, the Commercial Amphibian G-EAVE flown by Capt J E A Hoare, a Vickers Viking III and a Fairey III floatplane. The Beardmore W.B.IX and the Saunders Kittewake failed to make it.

Despite the competition being treated quite light heartedly by the manufacturers taking part, a great deal of useful testing was compiled. The Commercial Amphibian performed very well considering how quickly the machine was put together, coming second to the Vickers Viking, which took the first prize of £10,000. In fact, the Air Ministry thought the Commercial was such a good design that they raised the second prize from £4,000 to £8,000.

The Commercial's flying career was destined to be short as it was seriously damaged in an accident in October 1920. Not repaired, the design of the flying boat lived on by forming the framework for the Seal amphibian in 1921.

Production

One aircraft, G-EAVE, was built for the 1920 Air Ministry Competition for seaplanes and amphibians.

Technical data – Commercial Amphibian	
ENGINE	One 350hp Rolls-Royce Eagle VIII
WINGSPAN (Upper)	50ft
WINGSPAN (Lower)	47ft
LENGTH	32ft 6in
HEIGHT	14ft 6in
WING AREA	600 sq ft
EMPTY WEIGHT	3,996lb
LOADED WEIGHT	5,700lb
MAX SPEED	94.4mph
ALIGHTING SPEED	55mph
RANGE	312 miles at 80mph

The Commercial Amphibian pictured during the Air Ministry competition at Martlesham Heath in September 1920. Capt Hoare (third from left) is suitably attired in a fisherman's rig of heavy jersey and grey trousers. On arrival he was also wearing a Norfolk jacket, a tweed shooting hat and sea boots! (Via *Aeroplane*)

Sea King Mk I & Mk II

Development

Despite the requirement for the N.1B Baby expiring following the end of the First World War, Supermarine decided to continue to pursue the idea of a building a single-seat fighter flying boat. Several spin-off designs were created, including the Schneider Sea Lion, and by the time the aircraft made its public appearance at Olympia in July 1920, it was the only example of its type on display.

Design

The Sea King was single seat biplane powered by a 160hp Beardmore engine which first flew in early 1920. It was in this guise that the aircraft appeared at Olympia but, not long after, the engine was replaced by a 240hp Siddeley Puma.

By 1921, with R J Mitchell at the design helm, the Sea King was revised in response to the issuing of Specification N6/22, which called for a fighter that could operate from both the deck of a carrier or from water. The aircraft presented by Mitchell was the Sea King Mk II, which retained its single-seat and wooden hull but was also fitted with a retractable undercarriage and a fixed tail skid. The fin was much larger than the Mk I's and the tailplane was mounted half way up, rather than on top. Power was provided by a 300hp Hispano Suiza 8 engine.

Service

There are few details about the brief flying career of the Sea King Mk I but the Mk II is recorded as flying for the first time in December 1921. The Mk II proved to be an outstandingly manoeuvrable aircraft and its aerobatic ability was just as good as any landplane fighter of the day. The aircraft was very stable and the Mk II needed no trimming, regardless of whether the engine was running or not. There was also no sign of porpoising on the water and the Sea King Mk II could be flown 'hands off' in all but the most severe weather conditions.

Regardless, the Mk II was not selected for production but the Parnall Plover and Fairey Flycatcher, both capable of being fitted with either conventional undercarriage or floats were chosen, at first in limited numbers. The Flycatcher went on to be chosen by the Air Ministry.

Production

Only one high speed Mk I flying boat built. The single Mk II was a development of Mk I, which was converted to the Sea Lion II in 1922.

Technical data – Sea King Mk I and Mk II	
ENGINE	(I) One 160hp Beardmore or one 240hp Siddeley Puma (II) One 300hp Hispano-Suiza 8
WINGSPAN	(I upper) 35ft 6in (II) 32ft
WINGSPAN	(I lower) 30ft 5in
LENGTH	(I) 27ft 4in (II) 26ft 9in
HEIGHT	(I and II) 11ft 7in
WING AREA	(I) 339 sq ft
EMPTY WEIGHT	(II) 2,115lb
LOADED WEIGHT	(I) (Beardmore) 2,500lb (Puma) 2,646lb (II) 2,850lb
MAX SPEED	(I) (Beardmore) 110½mph (Puma) 121mph (II) 125mph at sea level
CLIMB	(II) 10,000ft in 12 min
ENDURANCE	(II) 2hrs

The Supermarine Aviation Works Ltd staff pose for a company photograph circa 1920, with the Sea King I providing part of the backdrop. (Via *Aeroplane*)

Seagull Mk I, Mk II & Mk III

Development

The development of the Seagull had already had its back broken thanks to its direct predecessor, the Seal Mk II. Further modifications would be carried out as the type evolved, creating just enough orders to keep Supermarine afloat until the arrival of the Southampton.

Design

The Seagull's roots were firmly planted within Seal Mk II N146, which was converted into the only Mk I. The conversion entailed a 480hp Napier Lion II engine, sturdier engine mounts, improved radiator shutters and wingtip floats plus modified ailerons.

By February 1922, a tentative order was placed by the Air Ministry for two more Seagulls, N158 and N159, which would become the first of 25 Mk IIs, which would become the first and main production model. The only significant difference with the Mk II was rearranged fuel tanks and a slightly more powerful 493hp Napier Lion IIB engine. A single Mk II, N9605, was rebuilt with a new tail with twin fins and rudders as well as Handley Page leading edge slots. It was unofficially designated as the Mk IV, although this has not been verified in surviving Supermarine records.

The final variant was unique to its customer, the RAAF. The Mk III was fitted with a 492hp Napier Lion V engine complete with tropical radiators. Six were supplied to the RAAF and a single Mk III was also delivered to Japan.

A single Seagull Mk II, N9644, was fitted with a Bristol Jupiter IX engine in a pusher arrangement in 1930. It would evolve into the Seagull Mk V, which would later change its name to the Walrus.

Operational Service

The first five production Seagull Mk IIs were selected to form 440 (Fleet Reconnaissance) Flight from personnel of 205 Squadron at Lee-on-Solent on 1 May 1923. Prior to this, another five Mk IIs were ordered in February, followed by 13 more in June. Six Mk IIs later served as carrier-based aircraft on HMS *Eagle* in the Mediterranean in 1925. The following year, one Seagull became the first British aircraft to be launched from a catapult by the RAE at Jersey Brow, Farnborough.

Six carrier-borne Seagull Mk IIIs were ordered for the RAAF in April 1925, serialled A91-1 to A9-6. All six were delivered by sea to Point Cook, Victoria, where they formed 101 Co-operation Flight on 30 June 1926. They later also served on HMAS *Albatross* from 1929 until they were replaced by Seagull Mk Vs. While the Australians enjoyed their Seagulls, the Royal Navy deemed the aircraft as having 'no potential naval use'.

Two Seagulls took part in the 1924 King's Cup Air Race and three ex-service machines were also placed on the British civilian register.

Production

32 aircraft built, made up a single Mk I, 25 Mk IIs, six Mk IIIs for Australia and a single machine exported to Japan.

Technical data – Seagull Mk I, Mk II and Mk III	
ENGINE	(I) One 480hp Napier Lion II (II) One 492hp Napier Lion IIB (III) One 492hp Napier Lion V
WINGSPAN	(I) 45ft 11in (II & III) 46ft
LENGTH	(I) 34ft 6in (II & III) 37ft 9in
HEIGHT	(I) 13ft 6in (II & III) 14ft
WING AREA	(I) 605 sq ft (II & III) 593 sq ft
EMPTY WEIGHT	(I) 3,691lb (II & III) 3,820lb
LOADED WEIGHT	(I) 5,462lb (II & III) 5,691lb
MAX SPEED	(I) 80mph at sea level (II) 80kts at 3,000ft, 79.8kts at 6,500ft (III) 85mph at sea level
CLIMB	(I) 3,000ft in 6.8 min (II) 3,000ft in 7 min 43 sec (III) 3,000ft in 7.67 min
CEILING	(I) 9,000ft (II & III) 9,150ft
ENDURANCE	(I) 3½hr (II & III) 4½hr
ARMAMENT	(I, II & III) One .303in Lewis machine-gun aft of the wings

Seagull Mk III N9647, one of several which helped to form 440 Flight at Lee-on-Solent on 1 May 1923. (Via Martyn Chorlton)

Seal II

Development

Following the excellent performance of the Commercial Amphibian in the 1920 Air Ministry Competition, a pair of prototypes was ordered, one from Supermarine and one from Vickers. The former would be called the Seal Mk II as the Commercial Amphibian was originally designated the Seal Mk I.

The prototype was given the serial N146 and on 25 November 1920, R J Mitchell had completed the first drawings.

Design

Mitchell designed the Seal Mk II to include all of the improvements highlighted in the post-competition report on the Commercial Amphibian. The Air Ministry needed the latest design to be a three-seat amphibian fleet spotter which was capable of landing on an aircraft carrier. To aid landing on a carrier's deck, the Seal Mk II needed a very low landing speed while still keeping the pilot in complete control.

The amphibian had a tractor layout and was powered by a liquid-cooled 450hp Napier Lion. The wings were required to fold back along the length of the fuselage and so not to protrude beyond the tail, the mainplanes were moved further forward than the Commercial Amphibian design. The pilot was positioned in the nose with his own, retractably mounted, Lewis machine gun. A wireless operator and a rear gunner were positioned aft of the mainplanes and no access to the pilot could be made because of the fuel tanks in the hull.

The hull was another Linton Hope design with a planing bottom and two steps. The hull was also broken down into watertight compartments to reduce the risk of sinking if an object was struck during landing or taking off.

Operational service

In May 1921, Seal Mk II N146 first took to the air in the hands of Henri Biard. At first, the Seal exhibited an uncomfortable yaw characteristic, which was eventually overcome by redesigning the fin, no less than three times.

Following a few weeks of flight trials, N146 was handed over to the RAF at Woolston on 2 June 1921. Following completion of its successful military trials, the Seal Mk II was converted to the Seagull Mk I.

Production

The original Seal Mk I was renamed the Commercial Amphibian, making the first Seal a Mk II. The Mk II became N146 before delivery to Grain. N146 was later converted to the Seagull Mk I while a single Seal was exported to Japan during 1922.

Technical data – Seal II	
ENGINE	One 450hp Napier Lion
WINGSPAN	46ft
LENGTH	32ft 10in
HEIGHT	14ft 10in
WING AREA	620 sq ft
EMPTY WEIGHT	4,100lb
LOADED WEIGHT	5,600ls
MAX SPEED	112mph
STALLING SPEED	55mph
CLIMB	10,000ft in 17 min
ENDURANCE	4hrs
ARMAMENT	Two .303 Lewis machine guns

The one and only Supermarine Seal Mk II N146, which was later converted into the Seagull Mk I. (Via *Aeroplane*)

Sea Eagle

Development

Once again, the legacy of the success of the Commercial Amphibian brought about another Supermarine design. The company had been studying the concept of how many passengers could be safely carried in an aircraft powered by a single-engine. This concept was partly in response to a new government policy that was looking at creating an official air route from Southampton to the Channel Islands and possibly France as well.

Air Ministry approval for such a route was given in June 1922 for an air service between Southampton, Cherbourg and Le Havre and a separate service to the Channel Islands under the guise of the British Marine Air Navigation Co. Ltd (BMAN).

Prior to this, R J Mitchell had already produced conceptual drawings for an enclosed cabin aircraft, capable of carrying six passengers. Powered by an Eagle engine in a pusher arrangement, the Sea Eagle had been born.

Design

The Sea Eagle biplane amphibian flying boat was powered by a single 360hp Rolls-Royce Eagle IX engine fitted with a four-blade pusher propeller. Passengers were carried in an enclosed forward cabin while the pilot and mechanic were accommodated in a cockpit above and behind it. To create more space in the hull, the fuel tank (later aircraft had twin tanks) were mounted on top of the upper mainplane, feeding the engine using gravity.

Service

Work had already begun on the first Sea Eagle when the Air Ministry announced that it would pay the BMAN a subsidy of £10,000 as well as a grant for £21,000 to pay of aircraft and spares. The aircraft would be three Sea Eagles purchased from Supermarine.

When the order was officially received, the three aircraft were registered as G-EBFK, G-EBGR and G-EBGS. The first aircraft made its maiden flight in early June 1923 and, by the following month, a CofA was issued after the aircraft passed its Air Ministry trials with flying colours.

On 25 September 1923, the first scheduled service between Woolston, which had now 'MARINE AIRPORT' painted across its main hangar, and Guernsey. The flight took on average, 1½ hours and a single fare cost £3.18s. G-EBGR and G-EBGS received their CofAs on 2 October and, days later, joined G-EBFK on the same route.

With the formation of Imperial Airways on 31 March 1924, the BMAN became one of several operations soaked up by the new airline. Imperial Airways continued to use the three Sea Eagles on the Guernsey route until 21 May when the fleet was reduced to two after G-EBFK crashed.

The service was suspended in the summer of 1925, only to be resumed with the two Sea Eagles in early 1926. A second Sea Eagle was lost on 10 January 1927 when G-EBGS was rammed by a ship in St Peter Port harbour, Guernsey. G-EBGR continued the route alone but was joined by Swan G-EBJY later in the year. By July 1928, Short Calcutta G-EBVG joined the route and eventually took over completely by October.

G-EBGR was withdrawn from use and the hull was preserved by Vickers until 1949. Later presented to BOAC, this unique piece of aviation history was burnt at Heston due to a lack of storage space.

Production

Three aircraft, G-EBFK, G-EBGR and G-EBGS all built for the British Air Navigation Co. Ltd in 1922/23. The first aircraft, G-EBFK, made its maiden flight in June 1923.

Technical data – Sea Eagle	
ENGINE	One 360hp Rolls-Royce Eagle IX
WINGSPAN	46ft
WINGSPAN (folded)	21ft 1in
LENGTH	37ft 4in
LENGTH (folded)	43ft
HEIGHT	15ft 11in
WING AREA	620 sq ft
EMPTY WEIGHT	3,950lb
LOADED WEIGHT	6,050lb
MAX SPEED	93mph at sea level
ALIGHTING SPEED	50mph
CLIMB	5,000ft in 19 min
RANGE	230 miles at 84mph

The second of three Sea Eagles built was G-EBGR, which was destined to be the only survivor once the type was retired in October 1928. The fuselage was later preserved and donated to BOAC in 1949 by Victor Paine (Hubert Scott-Paine's half-brother). At the time, it was the oldest British transport aircraft at the time, but this still not stop it from being destroyed at Heston in early 1954. (Via *Aeroplane*)

Scarab

Development

The Scarab was an amphibian flying boat based on the Seagull and Sea Eagle. Twelve Scarabs were ordered by the Spanish Naval Air Service in February 1924, the only operator to do so.

Design

The hull was, by now, a traditional Supermarine design, which was described as being very seaworthy. The cockpits, for example, always remained dry regardless of the conditions.

Power was provided by a single 360hp Rolls-Royce Eagle IX engine mounted below the upper mainplane with twin fuel tanks on top of the mainplane, just like the Seagull Mk III. The crew were all positioned in the front of the hull, the pilot located on the right hand side and furthest forward and a gunner behind him. At the rear was the navigator/wireless operator who had his own roomy wireless cabin. This crew layout was similar to the Channel and the Scarab and also had provision for dual-controls which could be fitted in the gunner's cockpit. The Scarab was also fitted with a retractable undercarriage, once again similar to that fitted to the Seagull.

Armament included a revolving mounting in the centre of the hull; fuel tanks were originally mounted in the same space in the Seagull, which could hold twelve 50lb bombs. The bombs were released down a tunnel and then out of the aircraft via an aperture in the bottom of the hull, which could be sealed off when landing on water.

Operational Service

The first Scarab, registered as M-NSAA, was first flown by Henri Biard on 21 May 1924. A week later, under full-load conditions, the Scarab was flown in front of Spanish officials as agreed in the original contract.

The Spanish spared no expense to take delivery of their new Scarabs and they had even commissioned the construction of a brand-new 10,000 ton seaplane tender. However, when Biard began landing next to the ship and the aircraft were craned aboard, the lift that was designed to take the Scarabs into the hold was found to be 4in short in one dimension. Whatever the Spanish crew tried to do, the Scarabs would not go down below and in the end all 12 machines were covered by tarpaulins and lashed to the deck, side by side with their wings folded.

En route, poor weather was encountered in the Bay of Biscay, battering the Scarabs with huge waves. No reports were received back in Britain as to how many of the Scarabs actually arrived in Spain in one piece. It is known that several took part in the Moroccan war not long after their arrival, all seeing action against Riff insurgents.

Production

Twelve Scarabs were ordered by the Spanish Government in February 1924 and after completion were registered as M-NSAA to M-NSAL.

Technical data – Scarab	
ENGINE	One 360hp Rolls-Royce Eagle IX
WINGSPAN	46ft
LENGTH	37ft
HEIGHT (tail down)	14ft 8in
WING AREA	610 sq ft
EMPTY WEIGHT	3,975lb
LOADED WEIGHT	5,750lb
MAX SPEED	93mph
LANDING SPEED	53mph
RANGE	Approx. 250 miles at 80mph
ARMAMENT	One free-mounted .303in Lewis machine-gun aft on Scarff ring in the rear cockpit. Up to 12 50lb bombs on a revolving mounting and/or four 100lb bombs under the wings

The first Scarab for the Spanish Naval Air Service pictured at Worthy Down in May 1924 being inspected by RAF officers and Spanish Officials. (Via *Aeroplane*)

Swan

Development

The story of the Swan began as far back as 1919, when design work began on a replacement for the Felixstowe F.5. Two ideas were explored; one was a military project, originally called the Shark torpedo carrier, which evolved into the Scylla. Simultaneously, a civilian version, intended for Instone Air Line, was called the Swan, although at first it was allocated the military serial N175.

Design

Ordered to specification 21/22, the Swan, designed by R J Mitchell, was destined to become the world's first twin-engine amphibian. The aircraft had equal-span two-bay wings which were designed to fold forward to minimize the amount of hangar space taken up. Power was provided by a pair of 360hp Rolls-Royce Eagle IX engines and, in the hands of Henri Biard it first flew on 25 March 1924. Mitchell originally designed the Swan as twelve-passenger amphibian, with passengers accommodated in the hull while the pilot and navigator sat in a raised cockpit above the fuselage to the rear of the passengers.

One of many novel features of the Swan was the undercarriage which was retracted when a fan, attached to a gearbox, was placed into the slipstream. The undercarriage was lowered by rotating the gearbox about its vertical axis. Prior to this, an undercarriage would have to be lowered manually by the pilot but with this system the gear could be lowered or retracted in approximately 30 seconds.

Service

Flight trials were extensive for the Swan and, before the aircraft was despatched to the MAEE at Felixstowe, the Eagle IXs were replaced with a pair of 450hp Napier Lion IIB engines. At the same time, the undercarriage was removed and the complex wing-folding was dispensed with and it was in this flying boat form that the aircraft underwent its military trials.

After successful testing, Mitchell redesigned the Swan by removing the large rear cockpit and re-positioning it in the nose of the aircraft. By February 1926, the aircraft had become the Swan Mk II ten-seat passenger flying boat and by now closely resembled a similar appearance to the later Southamptons.

Registered as G-EBJY, the aircraft was flown in its new form by Henri Biard on 9 June 1926. On board was F.J. Bailey, the manager of Woolston airport, eight young female employees of Supermarine and one representative from Imperial Airways. After a CofA was issued on 30 June 1926, the aircraft was loaned by the Air Ministry to Imperial Airways. The Swan flew services to the Channel Islands and, by 1927, was flying a regular service between Deauville, Le Touquet and occasionally Cherbourg. Sadly, its usefulness was short-lived and by the autumn of 1927 the aircraft was scrapped.

Production

One aircraft was ordered under contract 331411/22 for a commercial amphibian to specification 21/22 and given the serial N175, later re-registered as G-EBJY.

Technical data – Swan Mk I & Mk II	
ENGINE	Two 360hp Rolls-Royce Eagle IX and later two 450hp Napier Lion IIB
WINGSPAN	68ft 8in
LENGTH	48ft 6in
LENGTH (folded)	56ft
HEIGHT	18ft 3¼in
HEIGHT (folded)	26ft 1in
WIDTH (folded)	43ft 9in
WING AREA	1,264.8 sq ft
EMPTY WEIGHT	(Eagle) 7,800lb (Lion) 9,170lb
LOADED WEIGHT	(Eagle) 11,900lb (Lion) 12,832lb later rising to 13,710lb
MAX SPEED	(Eagle) 92mph (Lion/no undercarriage) 108½mph
CRUISING SPEED	83/87mph
LANDING SPEED	45/48mph
CLIMB	(Eagle) 5,000ft in 12 min (Lion) 10,000ft in 35 min 45 sec
CEILING	10,200ft

Swan N175 provides a wonderful backdrop during a visit by the Prince of Wales to the Supermarine Works in 1924. While the Prince was inspecting the flying-board, Henri Biard invited him aboard, a request he politely responded to by saying 'Not up that ladder – with this sword!' (Via *Aeroplane*)

Sparrow Mk I & Mk II

Development

A prize of £2,000 was put up by the Air Ministry in 1924 for the best British-designed lightplane that could be operated by flying clubs and private owners. During late September and early October that year, a contest called the Two-Seater Light Aeroplane Competition was held at Lympne in Kent to decide the winner.

Designed by R J Mitchell, Supermarine's entry was the first landplane that they had designed since the days of Pemberton-Billing.

Design

Sparrow Mk I

The Sparrow Mk I was designed and built for the 1924 Lympne light aircraft trials. It was a two-seat biplane powered by a 35 hp (26 kW) Blackburne Thrush piston engine, with dual control.

Built of wood, the two-seat fuselage was fitted with dual controls and was constructed with spruce longerons and covered in plywood. The wings were made up of a pair of spindled spars with built up ribs and separate nose ribs and were able to fold. The section of the upper wing was a modified Raf15 also known as the 'sloane' while the lower 'half' wing had a slimmer AD1 camber section. Steel tube interplane struts gave strength and full-span ailerons/flaps, which could be drooped to change the camber of the wing which gave excellent manoeuvrability and a wing loading of just 3½lb/sq ft.

The aircraft (registered G-EBJP) first flew on 11 September 1924. The Thrush, a three-cylinder 35hp radial engine, proved to be extremely unreliable and the Sparrow was eliminated from the light aircraft trial due to engine failure. In the Grosvenor Trophy Race at Lympne Aerodrome on 14 October 1924, it came fourth, with a speed of 62.08mph (99.91 km/h).

Sparrow Mk II

The aircraft was rebuilt for the 1926 Lympne Trials as a parasol monoplane (and redesignated the Sparrow II) and re-engined with a 32 hp (24 kW) Bristol Cherub III engine. During the trials, the Sparrow force-landed near Beachy Head on 12 September 1926, again being eliminated from the competition, which was won by the Hawker Cygnet. After use for testing wing sections, the aircraft was sold to the Halton Aero Club, remaining in existence until 1933.

Production

One aircraft, registered as G-EBJP and built for 1924 Air Ministry Aeroplane contest as No.'9', was entered as a sesquiplane. G-EBJP was then converted into a Mk II for the 1926 Two-Seater Light Aeroplane Competition but was unsuccessful in both events. It was later used for aerofoil trials and used under Air Ministry contract 730450/26/49.

Technical data – Sparrow Mk I and Mk II	
ENGINE	(Mk I) One 35hp Blackburne Thrush. (Mk II) One 32hp Bristol Cherub III
WINGSPAN (upper)	(Mk I) 33ft 4in (Mk II) 34ft
LENGTH	(Mk I) 23ft 6in (Mk II) 23ft
HEIGHT	(Mk I and II) 7ft 5in
WING AREA	(Mk I) 256 sq ft (Mk II) 193 sq ft
EMPTY WEIGHT	(Mk I) 475lb (Mk II Competition) 605lb
LOADED WEIGHT	(Mk I) 860lb (Mk II Competition) 1,000lb
MAX SPEED	(Mk I) 72mph, Mk II Raf 30) 65mph
LANDING SPEED	(Mk I) 27mph

The Sparrow Mk I having its wings unfolded at the Lympne Trials on 18 September 1924. R J Mitchell is second left.

S.4

Development

The idea to go ahead with revolutionary next stage in R J Mitchell's Schneider designs was a joint decision between Supermarine and Napier on 18 March 1925. This, in turn, was supported by the British government, which agreed to purchase the aircraft if success was achieved. The latest design was designated as the S.4, as Mitchell considered the racing Sea Lion Mk I, II and III as the S.1, S.2 and S.3.

Design and development

The S.4 was a stunning looking aircraft for the day with its streamlined fuselage, the cantilever monoplane was mounted on a pair of floats. The one-piece wooden framed wing was covered top and bottom with plywood, which increased in thickness from the tips to the centre. On the underside of each wing, a trough carried a water coolant pipe from the 680hp Napier Lion IV engine to Lamblin radiators, which were the only protrusions on the entire aircraft. Both ailerons and flaps were interconnected, the former being able to operate independently or in conjunction with the flaps, a feature that would not appear on subsequent S Series aircraft.

The three-section fuselage was made up of an all-metal forward fuselage and engine mounting, and a centre and rear section of semi-monocoque construction. The latter had not been seen since 1913 when the trophy was won by the Deperdussin. The floats were attached to fuselage by a pair of sloping A-frames and the single-piece wing passed through the fuselage and connected to the top of them. The engine was mounted on the forward A-frame.

Operational service

Given the registration G-EBLP, the S.4 was first flown by Henri Biard on 24 August 1925. Biard was destined never to be particular happy with the S.4, his main criticism being visibility. The cockpit was set so far back in the fuselage, Biard had several near misses with boats and ships, simply because he could not see them because of a huge blind spot created by the wing. Regardless, Biard stuck with the task and with little effort raised the world seaplane speed record to 226.752mph over Southampton Water on 13 September 1925.

Confidence was running high for a British victory in the S.4 or the Gloster III biplanes being entered for the forthcoming 1925 Schneider Trophy event being held at Bay Shore Park, Baltimore. Success for the Supermarine team, led by Capt C. B. Wilson, took an ominous turn when Biard slipped and hurt his wrist on the deck of the transport ship Minnewaska, during the trip across the Atlantic.

Conditions on arrival in Baltimore were not of a high standard and, with the aircraft housed in tents and poor weather complicating matters, there was little time for preparation before the race. During one particularly heavy storm, the tent housing the S.4 collapsed and a pole damaged the rear fuselage. The cold conditions also saw Biard catch the flu but this did not deter him from taking the S.4 out for test flight and practice session on 23 October. All seemed well as the S.4 flew as expected but as Biard began a high-speed run, the aircraft began to oscillate violently before he lost control and machine side-slipped into the bay from 200ft. Luckily, Biard survived the crash and was rescued after some time by fellow competitor Hubert Broad in his Gloster III. That year's Schneider was won two days later by Lt J Doolittle in a Curtiss R3C.

Production

N196-197 (2). Two aircraft were ordered under contract 618379/25 (25 August 1925) for the 1925 Schneider Trophy race, serialled N196 and N197. N197 was later allocated as G-EBLP while N196 was never built.

Technical data – S.4	
ENGINE	One 680hp (at 2,000rpm) Napier Lion IV
WINGSPAN	30ft 7½in
LENGTH (overall)	26ft 7¾in
LENGTH (fuselage)	25ft
HEIGHT	11ft 8½in
WING AREA	139 sq ft
WING LOADING	23lb per sq in
EMPTY WEIGHT	2,600lb
LOADED WEIGHT	3,191lb
MAX SPEED	226.75mph (World Seaplane Record)
ALIGHTING SPEED	85mph

The sole Supermarine S.4 at Calshot in August 1925. (Via Martyn Chorlton)

Southampton Mk I & Mk II

Development

Only surpassed by their length of service with the RAF by the Short Sunderland, the R J Mitchell-designed Southampton served for more than a decade. It was the first post-First World War design to enter service, taking over from the Felixstowe designs which dated back to 1917.

The prototype, N218 was a militarised development of the Swan amphibian, of which only one was built to Air Ministry Specification R.18/24. Only one Swan was ever built, but the Air Ministry were so impressed with it, they ordered Mitchells' follow-up design, the Southampton straight off the drawing board. Before details of the aircraft had been fully released, an initial production of six Mk Is had been placed.

History

This first batch were built with wooden hulls and wings with straight leading edges. The first production aircraft, N9896 made its first flight on 10 March 1925, and not long after, an additional order for 18 more Mk Is was placed. This was followed by an order for 41 Mk IIs, which differed from the Mk I by having duralumin hulls and more powerful 502hp Napier Lion VA engines. Approximately 28 Mk IIs had their wings modified with a slight sweep-back on the outer wing panels and all early aircraft built with wooden hulls were retrofitted with metal ones between 1929 and 1933.

Operational service

The Southampton first entered service with 480 (Coastal Reconnaissance) at Calshot in August 1925 and it was not long before the long-range flying boat began hitting the headlines. The first epic flight was a 10,000 mile 'cruise' around the British Isles followed by a 14,000 mile round trip flight to Egypt. The latter was flown from Plymouth in 1926 by Mk Is S1038 and S1039 and led by Sqn Ldr G Livock, a highly experienced flying boat captain who served for many years on the Felixstowes. This was surpassed by 205 Squadron, which was reformed with the Mk II at Seletar on 8 January 1929 from the Far East Flight. The same year, the squadron embarked on a 19,500 mile return journey from Singapore to Nicobar and the Andaman Islands. However, the longest and most famous of all Southampton flights was the 27,000 mile cruise by the Far East Flight led by Gp Capt H Cave-Brown-Cave CB, DSO, DFC. Four Mk IIs took part (S1149-S1152) in the flight from Felixstowe on 14 October 1927 to Singapore, via the Mediterranean and India, and a visit to Hong Kong.

68 Southamptons served with six RAF units, 201, 203, 204, 205, 209 and 210 Squadrons until December 1936 having carved a reputation for 'flying the flag' with unsurpassed reliability. Southamptons were also operated by other countries including Argentina, which operated eight (HB-1 to HB-8), all powered by Lorraine-Dietrich 12E engines and built by S. E. Saunders Ltd. The RAAF operated a pair of Mk IIs and the Danish and Japanese Navies flew one apiece. Turkey was the only other significant foreign operator with six (N3-N8), delivered in 1934.

Three aircraft were on the civilian register starting with Mk II ex-S1235, which was loaned to Imperial Airways by the Air Ministry in 1929. The single Mk II supplied to the Japanese Navy was converted to a 18-seat cabin airliner and used by Japan Air Transport and another sent to Japan, was registered as J-BAID and served with Nippon Kokuyuso Kenkyujo into the mid-1930s.

Production

Eighty-three Southamptons were built, made up of 79 production aircraft and four prototypes. This is broken down as 23 Mk Is with wooden hulls and Lion V engines; 39 Mk IIs with Lion Va engines; eight Mk IIs for Argentina with 12E engines, five of them with wooden and three with metal hulls and six Hispano-Suiza Mk IIs for Turkey.

Technical data – Southampton Mk II	
ENGINE	Two 500hp Napier Lion VA
WINGSPAN	75ft
LENGTH	49ft 8½in
HEIGHT	20ft 5in
WING AREA	1,448 sq ft
EMPTY WEIGHT	9,696.5lb
LOADED WEIGHT	15,200lb
MAX SPEED	95mph at sea level; 93mph at 2,000ft
CLIMB RATE	368 ft/min; 6,000ft in 29 min 42 sec
CEILING	(service) 5,950ft; (absolute) 8,100ft
RANGE	544 miles at 86mph at 2,000ft
ENDURANCE	6.3hrs

Right: The metal-hulled Southampton II S1149, which served as the flagship aircraft for the RAF Far East Flight, flown by Gp Capt H M Cave-Browne-Cave. (*Aeroplane*)

Below: The first of eight Southampton Is, HB-1 ordered for the Argentinian Navy on the step in the Solent. These flying boats were powered by Lorraine-Dietrich 12E engines. (Via *Aeroplane*)

Sheldrake

Development

A development of the Seagull, the Sheldrake came about from an original Spanish enquiry for an amphibian bomber. Drawings were first produced by Supermarine on 6 December 1923 and this hybrid design was actually meant to be the prototype of the earlier Scarab but was destined not to take to the air until 1927.

Design

In general, the Sheldrake resembled the Scarab with a few minor differences. The powerplant was a 450hp Napier Lion V and, rather than the gunners position being behind the pilot, a separate position was created behind the mainplane.

The extra 90hp the Lion engine provided pushed the Sheldrake along at 103mph, ten miles per hour quicker than the Scarab. There were no other major differences in performance.

Service

The lone Sheldrake was only ever seen once in public, displaying the number '17' for the Hampshire Air Pageant at Hamble on 12 May 1927. The Sheldrake was one of 20 different aircraft types that took part in a fly-past at the pageant.

Production

One aircraft was built under contract 466409/23, making use of a Seagull Mk II hull and serialled N180.

Technical data – Sheldrake	
ENGINE	One 450hp Napier Lion V
WINGSPAN	46ft
LENGTH	37ft 4½in
HEIGHT (tail up)	16ft 2½in
WING AREA	593 sq ft
EMPTY WEIGHT	4,125lb
LOADED WEIGHT	6,100lb
MAX SPEED	103mph at sea level
LANDING SPEED	55mph
RANGE	Approx. 250 miles at 85mph
ARMAMENT	One Vickers .303in machine-gun in nose and one Lewis .303in machine gun in the rear cockpit. Up to 1,000lb of bombs

The Supermarine Sheldrake, N180 was a shy public performer and was only seen on two occasions, both in 1927. (Via *Aeroplane*)

Sheldrake N180 taxiing at the Hampshire Air Pageant at Hamble in May 1927. (Via Martyn Chorlton)

Nanok

Development

The successful Southampton created a host of enquiries from overseas operators, including the Danish Navy, which requested a three-engined version capable of carrying torpedoes under the lower inner mainplanes. The layout had already been experimented with on Southampton N9900 and, initially, the concept seemed plausible.

Design

Following the order of a single prototype by Denmark on 17 June 1926 the aircraft was named 'Nanok', which was Danish for Polar bear. Delivery was expected to be achieved in under 12 months and the contracted price, minus the engines, was £10,000. The powerplant was to be a trio of 430hp Armstrong Siddeley Jaguar IVAs. Other than the additional engine, the general arrangement was no different than the Southampton Mk II, although performance was expected to be superior.

Service

Behind schedule, the Nanok, resplendent in Royal Danish Navy markings and registered as No.99, was first flown by Henri Biard on 21 June 1927. Initial flight testing showed the Nanok to be nose heavy, especially at low speeds. The problem was caused by the slipstream bypassing the horizontal tailplane but the fitment of an auxiliary all-flying elevator cured the anomaly.

It is not clear exactly when the Danes pulled out of the order but, in April 1928, the Nanok was being tested by the MAEE at Felixstowe. Here it was found to at least threemph down on the contracted speed, despite various modifications which had improved the original aircraft's performance. In the meantime, the Danish ordered a Jaguar VI-powered Southampton instead.

Production

Only a single Nanok was ever built, which was later converted to the luxurious private air yacht, the Solent.

The Nanok on the slipway at the MAEE at Felixstowe on 22 May 1928. (Via Martyn Chorlton)

Technical data – Nanok	
ENGINE	Three 430hp Armstrong Siddeley Jaguar IV
WINGSPAN	75ft
LENGTH	50ft 6in
HEIGHT	19ft 6in
WING AREA	1,571.8 sq ft
EMPTY WEIGHT	10,619lb
LOADED WEIGHT	16,311lb
MAX SPEED	113½mph at sea level, 101.2mph at 10,000ft*
STALLING SPEED	64mph
CLIMB RATE	607 ft/min; 5,000ft in 10 min 20 sec, 10,000ft in 31 min
CEILING	10,920ft
RANGE	240 miles 640 miles at 80mph
ARMAMENT	Two .303in Lewis machine-guns, one in bow and one amidships. Pair of 1,534lb torpedoes, under each mainplane
* These figures achieved with 10ft airscrews, replacing the original 9.625ft units	

Very rare photograph of the sole Nanok during flight trials. (Via *Aeroplane*)

S.5

Design

Following the failure of Britain to win the 1925 Schneider Trophy, a more serious approach was planned for the 1926 event. The Air Ministry would now play a bigger part in the development of high-speed seaplanes and, by the end of 1925, an order was placed for three aircraft from both Gloster and Supermarine with engines provided by Napier.

Various delays in completion and testing meant that entering the 1926 event could bring about the same result as the previous year so, to guarantee a victory, the 1927 event would be the new target. Thankfully, the Italians won the 1926 Schneider Trophy, stopping the United States from taking a third victory, which would have most likely ended the event.

Development

R J Mitchell had been working the new S.5 since the demise of its predecessor and, as a result, had gained a great deal of knowledge on how to improve his high-speed seaplane. However, the main problems that Mitchell faced were drag, weight and good performance on the water. Extensive wind-tunnel testing was available to both teams and three different versions of the S.5 were tested, including a gull-wing design.

A more conventional low-wing layout was adopted with a very slim all-metal duralumin semi-monocoque fuselage. The fuselage was so slim that there was no room for fuel but a 55 gallon tank was ingeniously placed in the starboard float. This also helped to cancel out the torque created by the direct-drive 875hp Napier Lion VIIA engine, lowering the centre of gravity and making the aircraft easier to handle on the water, especially during take-off.

The skin of the S.5 was made of light alloy plate while the rear fuselage and tail were almost the same as the S.4. The twin-spar wings were made of wood and incorporated the radiators, which covered the majority of both the upper and lower surfaces. This was a feature that created no drag compared to the older style Lamblin type.

Service

The first of the three S.5s built, N219 made its maiden flight on 7 June 1927 flown by Flt Lt O E Worsley. All three were ready for the next Schneider Trophy event, which was planned for Venice in late September, despite niggling problems with the Napier engines.

An exciting race began on 26 September, enjoyed by huge Italian crowds who still continued to cheer despite their own country's Macchi M.52s dropping out one by one through mechanical failure. This left Flt Lt S M Kinkead in the Gloster IVB, Flt Lt Worsley in N219 and Flt Lt S N Webster in N220 to fight for the finish. On the last lap, Kinkead had to retire, leaving the two S.5s to take first and second. Webster was the fastest in N220 with an average speed of 281.66mph, with Worsley second in N219 with an average speed of 271.01mph.

Sadly, Kinkead, an outstanding pilot, was destined to be killed in N221 during a world air speed record attempt on 12 March 1928.

As part of the RAF's High Speed Flight, S.5 N219 was also entered for the 1929 Schneider Trophy race and, in the hands of Flt Lt D'Arcy Crieg, finished a creditable third with an average speed of 282.11mph.

Production

The S.5s, N219, N220 and N221 were built to Air Ministry specification S.6/26. N219 ordered under contract 674204/26. N220 and 221, S.5 (modified) under contract 747192/27 for the 1927 Schneider Trophy race.

Technical data – S.5	
ENGINE	(N219) One 900hp (at 3,300 rpm) Napier Lion VIIA. (N220 & N221) One 875hp Napier Lion VIIB
WINGSPAN	26ft 9in
LENGTH (overall)	24ft 3½in
LENGTH (fuselage)	22ft ½in
HEIGHT	11ft 1in
WING AREA	115 sq ft
EMPTY WEIGHT	(N220) 2,680lb
LOADED WEIGHT	(N220) 3,242lb
MAX SPEED	319.57mph
ALIGHTING SPEED	85mph

Right: The first S.5, N219 is guided into the water at Calshot in July 1927. (*Aeroplane*)

Below: The third S.5 was N221, which did not take part in the 1927 Schneider Trophy race but was used by Flt Lt S M Kinkead in an attempt beat the World Air Speed Record. Sadly, Kinkead was killed in the attempt in the Solent, off Calshot, 12 March 1928. (*Aeroplane*)

Solent

Development

Following the rejection of the Nanok by the Royal Danish Navy, Supermarine found itself with an expensive flying boat that nobody wanted. However, after some clever marketing, the eyes of the Hon. A E Guinness were attracted to the idea of converting the Nanok into a luxurious 'air yacht' for his private use.

Design

Externally, other than the removal of the Danish serial No.99 and the British Civil Registration, G-AAAB being applied, the renamed Solent looked no different from the Nanok. Internally it was a different matter, as the hull was now fitted out with luxurious cabins capable of carrying up to 12 passengers.

Engines were the only subtle difference, being the 400hp Jaguar IVs rather than the original 430hp Jaguar IVs.

Service

The Solent was delivered to the Hon. A E Guinness on 7 August 1928. It's regular route was from the Hythe seaplane base on Southampton Water, to Dun Laoghaire harbour, County Dublin, and onwards across Ireland to Lough Corrib, not far from the owner's home in County Galway.

On 17 July 1931, the Solent was Wfu (withdrawn from use) and was scrapped in 1934.

Production

Only one Solent, c/n 1714, was built/converted by Supermarine.

Technical data – Solent	
ENGINE	Three 400hp Armstrong Siddeley Jaguar IVA
WINGSPAN	75ft
LENGTH	50ft 2in
HEIGHT	19ft
WING AREA	1,576 sq ft
EMPTY WEIGHT	9,840lb
LOADED WEIGHT	16,500lb
MAX SPEED	111mph at sea level
ALIGHTING SPEED	54mph
CLIMB RATE	5,000ft in 10 min
CEILING	11,000ft

The only Solent ever built was G-AAAB, which was delivered to the Hon. A E Guinness in August 1928. Withdrawn from use in July 1931, the luxury flying boat was scrapped in 1934.

The Solent being casted off for more flight trials. (Via *Aeroplane*)

Seamew

Development

It was Supermarine's idea to begin design work on a small shipborne amphibian back in 1924. By October, R J Mitchell had prepared the first of several drawings of an aircraft that resembled a scaled-down Southampton with three crew. In early January 1925, the aircraft was modified and, not long after, the drawings were presented to the Air Ministry, which promptly placed an order for a pair of prototypes.

Supermarine did not regard the order for two aircraft, now named the Seamew, with a great deal of urgency, as it was already busy producing the Seagull and the S.4 seaplane. Some progress was made in October 1925 on the drawing board but it was not until March 1926 that detailed working drawings were produced. However, by then, the S.5 and metal wings for the Southampton were seen as more important than embarking on a new, possibly non-profitable, project.

Finally, work began on the first Seamew, N212, in 1927, despite the amount of time Supermarine were spending on supporting the Southampton Far East Cruise.

Design

The Seamew featured a wooden hull, which was similar in construction to the Southampton and two-bay biplane wings, also made of wood but also a metal composite with a fabric covering. The tail unit had twin fins and rudders and power was provided by a pair of 238hp (at 2,100rpm) Armstrong Siddeley Lynx IV engines. The undercarriage was retractable, as befitting an amphibian, while the tailskid was fixed.

The pilot was positioned in a forward cockpit with a gunner behind him and a second gunner located behind the main plane.

Operational service

On 5 January 1928, the first Seamew N212 carried out its first engine runs, followed four days later by its maiden flight by Henri Biard. After early flight trials, plans were drawn up in March for more powerful engines and this gives the impression that the Seamew was underpowered. After two flight test trials carried out at Felixstowe during late 1928 and late 1929, the mainplane of N212 failed after just 65hrs and 50mins of flying. Problems had been experienced with the metal fittings in the wings of Southamptons and this failure on the Seamew may have not come as a complete surprise.

The second Seamew, N213, was fitted with four-blade propellers, unlike N212's two-bladed, in an attempt to solve the problem of water ingestion which was experienced by the first aircraft. N213 had an inferior climb rate to N212, purely because of the propellers, and the water ingestion problem could only be properly solved by reverting back to earlier design layouts of a single engine being protected by the hull from the sea. In highlighting this fact, the Seamew was an experimental success but was destined to be nothing more and both aircraft were quickly scrapped because of the fatigue and corrosion problems.

Production

Two aircraft, N212 and N213, were constructed under contract 60044/25 and specification 31/24.

Technical data – Seamew	
ENGINE	Two 238hp Armstrong Siddeley Lynx IV
WINGSPAN	45ft 11½in
LENGTH	36ft 5in
HEIGHT	15ft 1in
WING AREA	610 sq ft
SWEEPBACK	2°
EMPTY WEIGHT	4,675lb
LOADED WEIGHT	5,800lb
MAX SPEED	95mph at 2,000ft
CLIMB RATE	523 ft/min; 9,000ft in 22 min
CEILING	10,950ft
ARMAMENT	Two .303in Lewis machine-guns on mountings fore and aft of the mainplanes

The first Seamew N212 fitted with Armstrong-Siddeley Lynx engines and two-bladed propellers during flight trials at the MAEE, Felixstowe, on 31 October 1929.

S.6 & S.6A

Development

Despite the success achieved by the S.5 in the 1927 Schneider Trophy race, interest in the event began to slide, especially with regard to British government support. Pressure to produce a faster aircraft for each event was also taking its toll, although the Royal Aero Club did manage to persuade the FAI to stagger the race by two years, rather than one, to give time for the necessary development.

The extra time would prove very useful if Britain was going to deal with the increasingly stronger Italian team but, by 1928, the Napier Lion engine was not up to the challenge. Napier was awarded a contract to develop the Lion but refused, and an invitation by the Air Ministry to Rolls-Royce was offered instead. This was by far one of the most significant decisions in British aviation history.

Design

The production of the new Rolls-Royce engine is a lengthy story on its own but the bottom line was that R J Mitchell was hoping to receive a unit that could produce a minimum of 1,500hp; Rolls-Royce gave him the 1,900hp R engine. To say he was pleased would be an understatement and Mitchell was now imagining a seaplane that breached 400mph. While this figure would seem ambitious, it would be easily achieved less than seven years later in his outstanding Spitfire.

Designed specifically around the R engine, the S.6 was very similar in appearance to the S.5 but this time was completely built of light alloy with steel fittings. The wings were also similar to the S.5 although the radiators were made of 24-gauge continuous duralumin sheets instead of copper strips used on the previous design.

The fuselage was again a semi-monocoque, this time made up of 46 hoop frames, all held together by one longitudinal member on each side, extending from the engine bearers. The float struts were repositioned to cater for the bigger engine and the cowling was modified as well. Fuel was carried in both centre sections of the floats.

The S.6A came about as a backup plan for 1931 Schneider race, which saw both S.6s modified with new floats, extra cooling areas and balanced controls in support of the main competitors, the S.6Bs.

Operational service

In early 1929, the Air Ministry ordered four aircraft for the forthcoming Schneider Trophy race to Specification 8/28. Two S.6s, N247 and N48 from Supermarine under contract S27042/28 and a pair of VI monoplanes from Gloster.

The first S.6, N247 was virtually complete by 10 June and, eleven days later, the R engine was fitted and, by 3 July, the floats were fitted ready for weighing. Engines runs began on 30 July with no problems and on 5 August, N247 was delivered to Calshot. Five days later, N247 was flown for the first by Sqn Ldr A H Orlebar, the CO of the High Speed Flight and on 25 August, N248 had also successfully carried out its maiden flight.

Both S.6s performed outstandingly well during the 1929 Schneider Trophy race at Calshot. N247, the seaplane flown by Fg Off H R D Waghorn, came first at an average speed of 328.63mph. N248, flown by Fg Off R L R Atcherley, would have come second but turned inside one of the marker poles. However, Atcherley did manage to set new world closed-circuit records over 50 and 100km on laps six and seven, recording speeds of 332.49 and 331.75mph, respectively.

During the 1931 event, N247 was lost during training, killing Lt G N Brinton while N248 was held in reserve and did not race.

Production

Two aircraft, N247 and N248, were built to Air Ministry specification S.8/28 and ordered on 3 May 1929, under contract S27042/28. Both were later modified to S.6A under I.T.P. 30013/30 for the 1931 Schneider Trophy race. N248 is preserved at Solent Sky.

Technical data – S.6	
ENGINE	One 1,900hp (at 2,900rpm) Rolls-Royce R
WINGSPAN	30ft
LENGTH (overall)	25ft 10in
LENGTH (fuselage)	25ft 3in
HEIGHT	12ft 3in
WING AREA	145 sq ft
EMPTY WEIGHT	(S.6) 3,976lb. (S.6A) 4,471lb
LOADED WEIGHT	(S.6) 5,120lb. (S.6A) 5,771lb
MAX SPEED	357.7mph (World Speed Record)
ALIGHTING SPEED	95mph

Right: Supermarine S.6 N247 taxiing at speed. Getting the aircraft off the water amid all the spray proved troublesome. (*Aeroplane*)

Below: Supermarine S.6 N247, racing No. 2, was flown to first place in the 1929 Schneider Trophy contest by Fg Off HR Waghorn. The Officer Commanding the High Speed Flight, Sqn Ldr AH Orlebar, set a world absolute speed record of 357.7 mph in this machine on 12 September 1929, when this picture was taken. (*Aeroplane*)

Air Yacht

Development

Originating from military Specification R5/27 for a long-range reconnaissance flying boat for the RAF, the Air Yacht evolved into a luxurious aircraft which saw Supermarine produce its first multi-engine monoplane design.

Heavily influenced by the Dornier Wal, of which one example was being tested at nearby Calshot, the Air Yacht was constructed under a veil of secrecy at Woolston for a very wealthy private customer.

Design

The Air Yacht was a three-engined all-metal (duralumin and stainless steel fittings) high-wing monoplane with Saunders-Roe A.14 type hull, which had already been experimented with on Southampton N251. Devoid of wing-mounted floats, the Dornier influence of fitting large hull-mounted sponsons was applied to assist with hydro-dynamic lift during take-off. A braced tailplane with three vertical fins and rudders made the Air Yacht a very attractive machine for its day.

Power was provided by a trio of Armstrong Siddeley geared Jaguar VI engines, each developing 450hp. Each engine was neatly encompassed in a Townend ring fairing with long trailing exhaust pipes and two-blade wooden propellers.

The crew flew the aircraft from an open cockpit forward of the mainplane and behind this were two more open cockpits for occasional use by passengers or crew. Below, each cabin had its own hot and cold air ventilation system and the standard of finish throughout was as good if not superior to passenger aircraft of today. The owner's cabin had a bed, a small bath and a private toilet. Electric lighting was fitted throughout and the Air Yacht also had its own fully equipped galley. Cabins for the owner's guests also had their own wash basins, toilet and pantry, and between these and the owner's cabin, was a comfortable lounge area with settees, a sideboard and a folding table completed the fittings. All of this came at a cost, which, according to the original contract, was £35,000 but, by June 1931, had risen to £52,000, mainly attributable to the sumptuous interior.

Service

The Air Yacht's wealthy customer was the Hon. A E Guinness, who ordered the aircraft in 1929. The flying boat was first flown by Henri Biard in February 1930 but, for the remainder of the year, flew very little so it is presumed that it was during this period that the interior was fitted out.

It was not until 8 May 1931 that the Air Yacht was flown to Felixstowe for its airworthiness trials, by which time, the flying boat had been registered as G-AASE. Finally, a CofA was issued on 22 December 1931, but by this time the Air Yacht was rejected by Guinness in favour of a much smaller and less luxurious Saro Cloud.

After languishing at Hythe, the aircraft was purchased by a wealthy American lady, by the name of Mrs June J James in October 1932. The aircraft was then re-engined with three 525hp Panther IIA engines and renamed *Windward III* (it was originally called *Flying Oma*) in preparation for Mrs James embarking on cruises throughout the Mediterranean and beyond.

Unfortunately, the flying career of the Air Yacht was short and on 25 January 1933, the flying boat entered a flat stall off the island of Capri with Mrs James and a party on board. All escaped without serious injury and, after being rescued by a local fisherman, the Air Yacht was beached.

Production

One aircraft, G-AASE, designed at first for specification 4/27 for an armed reconnaissance seaplane. Completed as a luxury yacht for the Hon. A E Guinness and first flown in February 1930.

Technical data – Air Yacht	
ENGINE	Three 450hp Armstrong Siddeley Jaguar VI. Three 525hp Armstrong Siddeley Panther IIA
WINGSPAN	92ft
LENGTH	66ft 6in
HEIGHT	19ft
WING AREA	1,472 sq ft
EMPTY WEIGHT	16,808lb
LOADED WEIGHT	23,348lb
MAX SPEED	102kts at 2,000ft
CLIMB RATE	380ft/min
CEILING	6,500ft

Air Yacht G-AASE *Flying Oma* at Hythe pictured with its original Armstrong Siddeley Jaguar engines.

Southampton X

Development

The late 1920s was a very busy period for Supermarine with regard to flying boat development and, during 1929 alone, the company had five major projects in progress, including a potential replacement for the outstanding Southampton.

The aircraft would be known as the Southampton X but it bore no resemblance to its excellent predecessor. It had has been suggested that the name was only reused in an attempt to feed on the original aircraft's success. It would be a tough act to follow.

Design

The flying boat was a three-engine sesquiplane with a stainless steel hull built by Supermarine, while the wing, complete with engine mountings was constructed by Vickers at Weybridge. This split construction method came about because of the merger of Supermarine with Vickers (Aviation) in 1928. Both the wing and the hull were constructed over the original design weight and the performance of the Southampton X suffered as a result.

Power was initially provided by three Armstrong Siddeley Jaguar VIC engines but these would subsequently be changed in an effort to improve performance.

The design of the flying boat did prove that Supermarine's twin-engined layout was the way forward and this was shown with the later Scapa and Stranraer.

Service

Serialled N252, the Southampton X was flown for the first time from Southampton Water by Capt J 'Mutt' Summers in March 1930. Unsurprisingly, after flight testing at Felixstowe, the Southampton X was found to be a poor performer. This was because the original design empty weight was exceeded by over 3,000lb and the all-up weight by almost 4,000lb.

The original Jaguar VIC engines were not up to the job either and the fitment of a set of Panther engines did little to improve matters. Performance was improved when the Jupiter XFBM engines were fitted although the top speed of 130mph at 4,920ft was still 5mph below the original specification. This still meant that the Southampton X outperformed its main competitor, the Saunders-Roe A.7 Severn.

The Southampton X was also fitted with Jupiter XIF engines and modified with an enclosed cabin. It finally appeared with a set of Panther engines complete with Townend rings, repositioned outer interplane struts and small floats.

While the aircraft in its own right was a failure, it certainly helped Supermarine to steer back to the correct path for future aircraft production.

Production

One aircraft, N252, was ordered under contract 786295/27 (28 June 1928) as part of a contract that included three experimental Southamptons, N251-N253.

Technical data – Southampton X	
ENGINE	Three Armstrong Siddeley Jaguar VIC. Three Armstrong Siddeley Panther. Three 570hp Bristol Jupiter XFBM Three Bristol Jupiter XIF
WINGSPAN	79ft
LENGTH	55ft 6in
HEIGHT	21ft
WING AREA	1,235 sq ft
EMPTY WEIGHT	(Jaguar) 13,427lb. (Jupiter XFBM) 13,975lb
LOADED WEIGHT	(Jaguar) 21,117lb. (Jupiter XFBM) 23,000lb
MAX SPEED	(Jupiter XFBM) 130mph at 4,920ft
CLIMB RATE	(Jaguar) 5,000ft in 6 min. (Jupiter XFBM) 500 ft/min, 9,840ft in 18 min
CEILING	(Jaguar) 6,400ft (Jupiter XFBM) 11,800ft
RANGE	1,000 miles at 100mph
ARMAMENT	Three .303in Lewis machine-guns in bow and midships. 1,000lb of bombs on shackles below mainplanes

The only Southampton X, N252, at the point of taking-off from the Solent during early flight trials in April 1930. The aircraft is powered by Armstrong Siddeley Jaguar engines during this time. (*Aeroplane*)

S.6B

Development

The last of the historic line of Supermarine racing seaplanes almost never came about because of a u-turn in government support. Following the Wall Street Crash in 1929, official funding was removed, complete with a public statement that more than enough high-speed flight data had already been gleaned from the S.5 and S.6.

The Royal Aero Club, which would be organising the next Schneider Trophy Race in the Solent in 1931, set about discussing whether the British entry could be privately funded. The club concluded that it was not financially feasible and once its findings were published, the public response was, understandably, one of disappointment, especially as one more victory would secure the Schneider Trophy for Britain for good.

Lord Rothermere was always proactive with regard to aviation and, using his *Daily Mail* group of newspapers, began a public appeal that raised several thousand pounds. Further funding was secured from Lady Fanny Lucy Huston who publicly pledged £100,000, which suddenly made the government take notice. It was late in the day when the government u-turned again and announced in January 1931 that it would support a British entry to the race. In short order, the High Speed Flight was reformed and with only seven months to spare, Mitchell set about working on the next Supermarine seaplane.

Design

There was obviously no time to design and build a completely new aircraft so Mitchell's only option was to prepare a modified version of the S.6A, which was simply known as the S.6B. As few changes as possible were made, but the provision of a 2,300hp Rolls-Royce R engine made his task slightly easier. Modifications included making room for larger fuel and oil tanks, improvement of the engine coolant surface, better floats, statically balanced control surfaces, a new propeller, a slightly larger wing and increased strengthening and bracing to cover the extra weight. In similar fashion to the S.5, more fuel was carried in the starboard float than the port, to counter the torque of the powerful engine.

With regard to the cooling system, Mitchell referred to the S.6B as the flying radiator because of the total 'wetted' surface area of the aircraft, which was 948 sq ft., 470 sq ft was radiator surface that included the oil cooling.

Service

The two S.6Bs were given the serials S1595 and S1596, the former being flown for the first time by Sqn Ldr Orlebar on 29 July 1931. A huge amount of dedication had paid off to get both aircraft ready in time and included the efforts of Rolls-Royce who only achieved their own 'one-hour type test' of the R engine one week before the start of race on 12 September.

On the day of the Schneider Trophy, the race was a slight anti-climax as the Italians and French had both suffered setbacks and the United States was out of contention. This left the trophy for the taking but the S.6Bs were still determined to put on a show and win the trophy in style.

Delayed by one day through poor weather, the 'race' was flown on 13 September, beginning with S1595 flying the course on its own. Flt Lt J Boothman completed the course in 340.8mph, winning the

Schneider Trophy outright, which became, and still remains, the property of the Royal Aero Club. S.6B S1596 then taxied out to make an attempt on the World Air Speed Record, which Flt Lt G Stainforth achieved with a speed of 379.05mph.

Before the High Speed Flight was disbanded again, a final reprieve saw the 400mph barrier broken for the first time by Flt Lt G Stainforth in S.6B S1596 on 29 September, reaching a speed of 407.5mph.

Production
Two aircraft, S1595 and S1596, specifically built for the 1931 Schneider Trophy race.

Technical data – S.6B	
ENGINE	One 2,350hp (at 3,200 rpm) Rolls-Royce R
WINGSPAN	30ft
LENGTH (overall)	28ft 10in
LENGTH (fuselage)	25ft 3in
HEIGHT	12ft 3in
WING AREA	145 sq ft
EMPTY WEIGHT	(S1595) 4,590lb
LOADED WEIGHT	(S.6A) 6,086lb
MAX SPEED	407.5mph (World Speed Record). 300mph in level flight
ALIGHTING SPEED	95mph

Above left: Flt Lt Boothman (centre) with High Speed Flight mechanics after winning the Schneider Trophy at Calshot in1931 in S.6B S1595 at an average speed of 340.8 mph. (*Aeroplane*)

Above right: S.6B S1596 being checked over on the slipway at Calshot prior to entering the 1931 Schneider Trophy Air Race. (*Aeroplane*)

Scapa

Development

Following the experience gained, good and bad, from the three-engined Southampton X, R J Mitchell wisely returned to the tried and tested design philosophy of the Southampton. Resources offered by the recent merger with Vickers gave Mitchell access to additional technical facilities, both aerodynamic and hydrodynamic, which helped to improve the design of the hull and refine drag characteristics of the superstructure.

Design

A prototype, known as the Southampton IV, was designed to Air Ministry Specification R.20/31 which was received in November 1931. The flying boat was of similar size and layout to the Southampton but incorporated a host of improvements.

The structure of the hull was metal throughout while the wings and tail surfaces were also metal but fabric-covered. The tail, which bore a passing resemblance to the Southampton, had two fins rather than three.

Power was provided by a pair of 525hp Rolls-Royce Kestrel IIIMS, which were mounted in aerodynamically designed nacelles and positioned below the upper mainplane. This also helped to improve the aerodynamic efficiency of the usually cluttered centre section.

The crew, starting with the two pilots, were provided with an enclosed cockpit plus three air gunners positions, one in the nose and two staggered aft of the mainplane.

Operational service

The prototype Southampton IV S1648, renamed Scapa in October 1933, was first flown by 'Mutt' Summers on 8 July 1932. Forty test flights were carried out by Supermarine before the aircraft was sent to Felixstowe for service trials on 29 October. One test included a ten-hour nonstop flight over the North Sea and, in November, the flying boat was sent Malta for further trials with 202 Squadron. The Scapa was chosen to re-equip 202 Squadron at Kalafrana, which it joined in May 1935. The type also joined 204 Squadron at Aboukir and Alexandria where, together with 202 Squadron, the Scapas carried out anti-submarine patrols throughout the Spanish Civil War to protect neutral shipping. 204 Squadron had been in the region since September 1935 in response to the potential posed from the Italians who had just invaded Abyssinia. By August 1936, they had returned to Mount Batten.

In a time-honoured tradition, the Scapa also took part in several long-distance cruises, including a 9,000 mile round trip to Nigeria, via Algiers, Gambia and Lagos in 1936 flown by 202 Squadron.

At home, Scapas also joined 228 Squadron at Pembroke Dock and 240 Squadron at Calshot where the latter served the longest, being replaced by Singapores in December 1938. However, several served on into 1939.

Production

Fifteen Scapas were produced in two batches of 12 and the three, including the prototype Southampton IV.

Technical data – Scapa	
ENGINE	Two 525hp Rolls-Royce Kestrel IIIMS
WINGSPAN	75ft
LENGTH (on chassis)	53ft
HEIGHT (on chassis)	21ft
WING AREA	1,300 sq ft
EMPTY WEIGHT	10,030lb
LOADED WEIGHT	16,080lb
CRUISING SPEED	123mph
MAX SPEED	142mph at 3,280ft
ALIGHTING SPEED	64mph
CLIMB RATE	625 ft/min. 9,840ft in 20 min
CEILING	15,500ft
RANGE (max)	1,000 miles with 2,650lb military load at 100mph at 5,000ft
ARMAMENT	Three .303in Lewis machine-guns, one in bow and two amidships. 1,000lb of bombs carried under mainplanes

Excellent view of the prototype Southampton IV, later Scapa I S1648, showing how uncluttered the engine layout and wing design was, compared to earlier Supermarine designs. (*Aeroplane*)

K4200, the last aircraft of the first production batch of 12 machines, being launched at Woolston for the first time on 30 October 1935. It was delivered to 204 Squadron the same day. (*Aeroplane*)

Seagull V

Development

The story of the Seagull Mk V began in 1930 when Seagull Mk II, N9644, was modified with a Jupiter engine driving a pusher propeller and redesignated as the Mk III. While the original Seagull would never be robust enough to stand being catapulted from a warship, an aircraft with a similar arrangement and a stronger construction would.

Also in 1930, there was still a naval requirement for a single-engine reconnaissance amphibian, which R J Mitchell designed as the Supermarine Type 181. Two versions, one a pusher and the other a tractor arrangement were specifically aimed at an Australian requirement but, at the time, no interest was shown in the project and Supermarine concentrated its efforts on the Schneider seaplanes.

Design

In 1932, Mitchell returned to the Type 181 but created a new design called the Type 223, which quickly reached the model stages and testing in Vickers' own water tank in St Albans. The design was offered directly to the RAAF as private venture because the Royal Navy had shown no interest in the type. Luckily for Supermarine, the Australians were keen to see more details of the new aircraft.

The Type 223 was constructed of both wood and metal; for example, the wings were made up of stainless steel front and rear spars with tubular flanges and corrugated webs with spruce and plywood secondary members. The horizontal stabiliser was constructed in a similar way while the fin was integrated into the hull with the rudder made entirely of wood.

The hull was a one-step design. It was the first time Supermarine had used the concept, which was heavily influenced by a design draughtsman who had joined Supermarine from Canadian Vickers. The hull was made entirely of light alloy and was skinned with flat plates to speed up production and make repairs easier.

The engine, which was initially a Pegasus Mk IIL2P, was mounted in a streamlined nacelle above the hull and drove a four-blade propeller. The slipstream from the engine caused a yawing effect but, by angling the Pegasus three degrees to starboard, the problem was solved and this solution was retained in all Seagulls and subsequent Walrus production.

Fuel tanks were positioned in the upper wings, outboard of the centre section with a capacity of 122 gallons which was later increased to 155 gallons. The crew, which was usually three for a Seagull V comprising a pilot, navigator and wireless telegraphist. Gun positions were in the nose and aft of the lower mainplane, the former having a retractable .303 Vickers K mounted on a Scarff ring.

Operational service

The Type 228 Seagull V, with prototype number N.1 was first flown by 'Mutt' Summers from Southampton Water on 21 June 1933. Just five days later, the aircraft was performing at the second SBAC show at Hendon and, much to R J Mitchell's surprise, Summers looped the Seagull with little effort.

After a host of trials with the MAEE and RAE, the RAAF placed an order for 24 aircraft on 24 August 1934. The first of these, A2-1, made its first flight on 25 June 1935, and after teething troubles were ironed out the Seagull was delivered direct to HMAS *Australia* at Spithead on 9 September. The second aircraft, A2-2, was delivered to HMAS *Sydney* and the remainder were shipped for service with No.1 Seaplane Training Flight at Point Cook, Victoria, and late 101 Flight, RAAF at Richmond, New South Wales. The type served the Australians until 1943.

Production

The RAAF ordered 24 Seagull Vs under specification 6/34 with serials A2-1 to A2-24. Two aircraft, A2-3 and A2-4, were transferred to the Australian civil register as VH-BGP and VH-ALB, respectively. The latter is today preserved in the RAF Museum at Hendon.

Technical data – Seagull V	
ENGINE	One 625hp Bristol Pegasus IIM2
WINGSPAN	46ft
LENGTH (on chassis)	38ft
HEIGHT (on chassis)	15ft
WING AREA	610 sq ft
EMPTY WEIGHT	4,640lb
LOADED WEIGHT	6,847lb
MAX SPEED	125mph at 3,280ft
ALIGHTING SPEED	54mph
CLIMB RATE	900 ft/min 10,000ft in 17 min 15 sec
CEILING	15,500ft
RANGE	634 miles at 95mph
ARMAMENT	Two Vickers K machine-guns in bow and amidships

The prototype Seagull V, which later gained the serial K4797, was used very effectively to convince the Air Ministry that the type would be both useful to the Royal Navy and the RAF. In April 1935, the Air Ministry placed an order for a dozen Seagull Vs that saw their names changed to Walrus before construction was completed. (Via Martyn Chorlton)

Type 224 F.7/30

Development

The Type 224 was designed and built in response to Air Ministry Specification F.7/30, issued in October 1931, which required an all-metal single-seat day and night fighter capable of 250mph and fitted with four machine guns to replace the Gloster Gauntlet. The hotly contested competition to win the order saw seven other designs entered, all confident that their fighters had the manoeuvrability and long endurance, low landing speed, steep initial climb and good visibility for the pilot was also required of the specification.

Design

R J Mitchell was very keen to apply all of the knowledge gained from the Schneider machines and previous flying boat types to produce a landplane fighter, which was no easy task.

Another factor to the success or failure of the Type 224 was that the Air Ministry were happy for any powerplant to be used but would prefer an aircraft fitted with the Rolls-Royce Kestrel (later Goshawk II) IV engine, which was cooled by evaporation. The concept of this system was that water was boiled first and condensed into steam rather than cooling the water before it boiled as with a normal radiator, therefore saving weight by carrying less water. Depending on the position of the header tank and condenser the system could work well. In the case of the Type 224, the leading edges of the wings were used as condensers, in the same way that the S series aircraft had been designed.

The Type 224 was a very clean looking aircraft with a monocoque fuselage and with inverted gull-wing layout. This wing design was selected to reduce the length of the fixed undercarriage legs and in turn reduce drag. Known to be laterally unstable, the gull-wing was extensively wind tunnel tested and this revealed that the Type 224 was directionally unstable as well. A large fin solved the later problem and the wind-tunnel facilities were also used to full effect on a full-scale model of the open cockpit to make sure that the pilot was to not exposed to buffeting.

The wing was made up of a single forward main spar with the cooling condensers attached to the forward edge along its entire length, which joined to produce a very rigid 'D-box'. To the rear of the main spar the wing was covered in fabric.

A pair of .303in machine guns were positioned either side of the cockpit and another pair, one on each side, was located in the large 'trouser' fairings that concealed the main landing gear.

Service

On 19 February 1934, the Type 224, which was unofficially called Spitfire, was flown for the first time by 'Mutt' Summers. Performance was found to be very disappointing and the predicted maximum speed of 245mph was missed by 20mph; the climb to 15,000ft also took three minutes longer than intended. In the end it was a direct development of the Gauntlet, namely the Gladiator, which appeared as a late contender for F.7/30, having only made its maiden flight in September 1934.

Mitchell was not at all disheartened by the outcome of the F.7/30 competition and great deal of good data came from the exercise. All of the data would prove useful in the massive leap in design and technology that Supermarine would make in preparation for its next Spitfire.

Production

One aircraft, K2890, was built under contract 189222/32 and specification F.7/30.

Technical data – Type 224	
ENGINE	One 600hp Rolls-Royce Goshawk II
WINGSPAN	45ft 10in
LENGTH (tail-up)	29ft 5¼in
HEIGHT (tail-up)	11ft 11in
WING AREA	295 sq ft
EMPTY WEIGHT	3,422lb
LOADED WEIGHT	4,743lb
MAX SPEED	228mph at 15,000ft
LANDING SPEED	60mph
CLIMB	15,000ft in 9½ min
CEILING (absolute)	38,800ft
ARMAMENT	Four .303in machine-guns, two in fuselage and two in wing roots, synchronised to fire through propeller

'Mutt' Summers taxies Type 224 K2890 '2' to the 'New Types Park' at the RAF Display at Hendon on 30 June 1934. (Via *Aeroplane*)

Walrus Mk I & Mk II

Development

Originally designed as nothing more than a private venture amphibian capable of being catapulted from warships, the Walrus went on to blossom becoming one of the greatest aircraft of World War Two. Almost overlooked by the Royal Navy and not even considered by the RAF, it was the crucial order by the RAAF for two dozen Seagull Vs that helped to raise the profile of this great little aircraft, which was named Walrus by the RAF from August 1935.

Design

The design of the Walrus is covered in more detail in the Seagull V chapter, as there were very few differences. The Walrus Mk I had a metal hull and was powered by a 750hp Pegasus VI while the Mk II was built with a wooden hull was powered by the same unit but developed 775hp.

Operational service

The Air Ministry placed the first of many orders for 12 Walrus Mk Is (K5772-K5783) in May 1935 to Specification 2/35, the first of which flew on 18 March 1936. By late 1939, Supermarine had already built 285 but was forced to transfer Walrus production to Saunders-Roe in 1939 to make way for the Spitfire.

All of these early Walruses were delivered to the FAA, and examples could be found serving with the following units; 700, 701, 702, 710, 711, 712, 714, 715, 716, 718, 720, 722, 728, 730, 733, 737, 740, 742, 743, 747, 749, 751, 754, 757, 763, 764, 765, 771, 772, 773, 777, 778, 781, 782, 783, 787, 788, 789, 796, 836 and 1700 Squadrons. From October 1941, the Walrus became a valuable addition to the RAF inventory and by the war's end approximately 250 had been transferred from Royal Navy contracts. The first RAF Walrus joined 275 Squadron at Valley and 278 Squadron at Matlaske in the air-sea rescue role. Hundreds of aircrew owed their lives to be rescued by a 'Shagbat', an often dangerous occupation for the Walrus crew, which only in recent years has warranted any kind of historical or official recognition. 277 Squadron rescued 598 personnel from the 1,000 picked up around the British Isles. The Walrus served with the following RAF units until April 1946; 89, 269, 275, 276, 277, 278, 281, 282, 283, 284, 292, 293, 294 and 624 Squadrons.

The Walrus also served in Argentina, Ireland, the Royal Canadian Navy, the RNZAF and Turkey.

Production

There were 746 Walruses built; 191 of them were Mk IIs (wooden hull), the majority of which were built by Saunders-Roe, which produced 461 aircraft. RAF and Royal Navy aircraft were produced in 12 batches from 1936 to 1944.

Technical data – Walrus 1	
ENGINE	One 750hp Bristol Pegasus VI
WINGSPAN	45ft 10in
LENGTH (on chassis)	37ft 7in
HEIGHT (on chassis)	15ft 3in
WING AREA	610 sq ft
EMPTY WEIGHT	4,900lb
LOADED WEIGHT	7,200lb
MAX SPEED	135mph at 4,750ft
ALIGHTING SPEED	57mph
CLIMB RATE	1,050 ft/min. 10,000ft in 12 min 30 sec
CEILING	18,500ft
RANGE	600 miles at 92mph
ARMAMENT	Two Vickers K machine-guns in bow and amidships

The very first production Walrus Mk I K5772 at the MAEE, Felixstowe, for performance trials in March 1936

For a stranded airman, the sight and sound of a Walrus approaching must have been a heartwarming experience. This 276 Squadron Walrus demonstrates how it was done. (*Aeroplane*)

Stranraer

Development

It was while the specification was being written for the Scapa that the Air Ministry issued another requirement for a general purpose coastal patrol flying boat able to carry a 1,000lb military load over 1,000 miles. An ability to maintain flight on a single engine with 60% of the fuel load still on board was another requirement. The Scapa was unable to achieve any of this which was encompassed in Specification R.24/31. So Supermarine decided to design a scaled up Scapa called the Southampton V (renamed the Stranraer in August 1935), making the company's latest product a restricted development version of its predecessor.

Design

The wing span, area and weight of Stranraer were 12% bigger than the Scapa. The rudders were the same size but the elevators were 7% greater than the Scapa's with larger aerodynamic balances. The trim tabs were large enough to keep the aircraft straight and level with one engine shut down.

The chosen powerplant was, at first, the Kestrel but the Bristol Pegasus IIIM was chosen instead for the prototype and the eventual production aircraft were fitted with the capable 920hp Pegasus X. The engines were mounted under the top wings and, being air-cooled, lacked the clutter of radiators and their pipework. Fuel was carried in the upper centre section and oil tanks and their coolers were fitted in the leading edge of the wing.

The hull had a cross-section 18% larger than the Scapa's but was found to be just as efficient in the water after tank tests at St Albans. The forward gun was retractable and the enclosed cabin for the pilots flowed back along the fuselage, rather than being dipped as in previous designs. A second gun position was located behind the lower mainplane and the tail gunner had his own faired position in a raised copula behind the twin fins.

Operational service

The Air Ministry placed an order to Specification 17/35 in August 1935 for 17 aircraft, despite originally rejecting the Stranraer in favour of the SARO London. The Stranraer Mk I first entered RAF service with 228 Squadron at Pembroke Dock in April 1937. In September 1939, 15 were still in service, despite the arrival of the Sunderland, all serving from Scottish bases with 209 and 240 Squadrons. By April 1941, the flying boat was withdrawn from front-line service, but a few continued in the second line until late 1942.

The Stranraer actually served in greater numbers with the RCAF, many of 40 built by Canadian Vickers until 1946. Units included No.4(BR), 5(BR ex-GR), 6(BR), 7(BR), 9(BR), 117, 120 and 166 Squadrons, RCAF.

Production

A total of 58 Stranraers were built starting with the prototype K3973, ordered under contract 262922/33. The first and main production batch for the RAF was for 17 aircraft (K7287-K7303) ordered in 1935, which was followed by an additional order for six more in May 1936, but the latter was cancelled.

Canadian Vickers production of the Stranraer amounted to 40 aircraft for the RCAF in the serial ranges 907-916, 918-923, 927-938 and 946-957. 14 of these went on to serve on the Canadian civilian register, the last of them retiring in 1957. Ex-920, which became CF-BXO, is today preserved at the RAF Museum, Hendon.

Technical data – Stranraer	
ENGINE	Two 920hp Bristol Pegasus X
WINGSPAN	85ft
LENGTH (on chassis)	53ft 10in
HEIGHT (on chassis)	21ft 9in
WING AREA	1,457 sq ft
EMPTY WEIGHT	11,250lb
LOADED WEIGHT	19,000lb
MAX SPEED	165mph at 6,000ft
ALIGHTING SPEED	58½mph
CLIMB RATE	1,350 ft/min. 10,000ft in 10 min
CEILING	18,500ft
RANGE	1,000 miles at 105mph at 5,000ft
ARMAMENT	Three .303in Lewis machine-guns, one in bow, amidships and tail. 1,000lb of bombs carried under mainplanes and eight 20lb bombs in bays in underside of lower mainplanes

The prototype Stranraer (ex-Southampton V), K3973, undergoing flight trials with the MAEE at Felixstowe in November 1934. Apart from a brief spell with 210 Squadron, the aircraft only flew with the MAEE and Supermarine before being SOC on 30 October 1938. (*Aeroplane*)

The pilot of an RCAF Stranraer concentrates as he enters a turn, photographed from the gunner's position in the nose. (Via *Aeroplane*)

Spitfire Mk I, IA & IB

Development

The foundations of a truly remarkable aircraft that would remain in production for 11 years, remain in front line service for the whole of World War Two and total more than 22,000 built in 33 different variants were laid by R J Mitchell in 1934.

Mitchell had already been encouraged to redesign the Type 224 but, during 1934, two events took place that would change his approach for the better. The first was the issue, by the Air Ministry, of Specification F.5/34 for a new fighter fitted with eight machine guns. Following the problems being encountered by the Goshawk engine, the specification was modified to F.36/36 for the same armament and the use of the new Rolls-Royce PV-12 engine, which later became the iconic Merlin. The engine would produce 1,000hp giving Mitchell all he needed to produce something very special.

Design

The fuselage of the Spitfire was a stressed skin construction with an oval cross-section. Made up of four main longerons, the skin was made of Aclad, which was riveted to 15 channel-section frames. The fin was integral and detachable, being held in place by 52 bolts. The forward five frames were u-shaped and, within this area, the fuel tanks were positioned and then behind them the cockpit.

The stress-skinned wings were built separately and were an elliptical structure, each having a single main spar and a second auxiliary spar. They were attached to the fuselage by the main spars at the fire-proof bulkhead and the auxiliaries at frame ten, the latter with just a single bolt. Control surfaces were initially fabric-covered but later were metalled.

The undercarriage was cantilevered, retracting outwards into the underside of the wing, at first by a hand-pump and then later on by an engine-driven pump.

The prototype, K4054, was hand-built, differing in many ways from the later production machines. On 5 March 1936, with its undercarriage locked down, the Spitfire made its first flight from Eastleigh, flown by 'Mutt' Summers who after landing made the historic remark, 'Don't touch anything'.

Operational service

On 3 June 1936, the Air Ministry placed the first of many production contracts for 310 Spitfire Mk Is, with a planned completion date of March 1939. The complexities of the fighter compared to the Hurricane caused production delays but Supermarine prevailed, delivering the last of the first batch by September 1939. One month later, Supermarine had contracts in place to produce another 4,000!

The Spitfire Mk I entered service with 19 Squadron at Duxford on 4 August 1938, and, by the beginning of World War Two, Fighter Command fielded nine operational Spitfire squadrons.

The Mk I was bloodied for the first time on 16 October 1939, much to the annoyance of the regulars as the first kills were claimed by a pair of auxiliaries, namely 602 and 603 Squadrons. A pair of Ju88s were brought down over the Firth of Forth by 602 and a He111 was shot down into the North Sea by 603 Squadron. Just 12 days later, the two Scottish-based squadrons shared an He111, which crashed near Dalkeith, thus claiming the first aircraft shot down over Great Britain since the First World War and the first German aircraft to be brought down on British soil, all in less than a fortnight.

By July 1940, Fighter Command had 19 Spitfire squadrons prepared for the Battle of Britain in which the fighter's performance has gone down in the annuls of history.

The Mk I served with the following RAF units, 19, 41, 54, 64, 65, 66, 72, 74, 92, 111, 118, 122, 123, 124, 129, 131, 132, 140, 145, 152, 222, 234, 238, 249, 257, 266, 303, 308, 313, 403, 411, 452, 457, 485,

501, 510, 602, 603, 609, 610, 611 and 616. The Mk I also equipped the following FAA units, 748, 759, 761, 762, 775, 791, 794, 880 and 897 Squadrons.

Production

There were 1,567 Mk Is built in six production batches plus the prototype, K5054, which was ordered to specification F.37/34 under contract 361140/34 on 1 December 1934. Of these, 1,517 were built by Supermarine between May 1938 and March 1941 and 50, ordered as Mk IAs, were built by Westland Aircraft, Yeovil, between July and September 1941.

Technical data – Spitfire Mk I	
ENGINE	(I) One 1,030hp Rolls-Royce Merlin II. (IA & IB) One 1,030hp Rolls-Royce Merlin III
WINGSPAN	36ft 10in
LENGTH	29ft 11in
HEIGHT (prop vertical, tail down)	11ft 5in
WING AREA	242 sq ft
TARE WEIGHT	4,341lb
LOADED WEIGHT	5,800lb
MAX SPEED	364mph at 18,500ft
CLIMB	20,000ft in 9.4 min
RATE OF CLIMB (initial)	2,530 ft/min
RANGE	395 miles at cruising speed of 210mph
CEILING (service)	31,500ft
ARMAMENT	(I early) Four .303in machine-guns. (I & IA) Eight .303in machine-guns. (IB) Two 20mm guns

Above left: Pristine line of Spitfire Mk Is belonging to 19 Squadron at Duxford in May 1939. The squadron code 'WZ' was only used from October 1938 to September 1939. (*Aeroplane*)

Above right: The prototype Spitfire K5054 after being modified to Mk I standard with Jeffrey Quill at the controls. (*Aeroplane*)

Sea Otter Mk I & Mk II

Development

R J Mitchell wasted no time in designing a successor to the Walrus, even before the first production example had flown. The Sea Otter, which was originally referred to as the Stingray, was designed in accordance with Air Ministry requirements that included an increase in loaded weight, equipment to be the same for either cruiser or carrier operations, dive-bombing capability, a greater range and a limited span of 46ft. On submitting cost figures, drawings and technical information, the Air Ministry gave Supermarine the green light to proceed in April 1936, allocating the serials K8854 and K8855 to a pair of prototypes.

Design

Built to Specification 5/36, the dimensions were similar to the Walrus and construction methods were also the same. The main difference between the Walrus and the Sea Otter was the position of the power plant, which, in the latter's case, was in the tractor position, rather than the pusher. After pondering between a Bristol Aquila or Perseus engine, a 796hp Mk VI version of the latter was chosen, fitted with a two-blade propeller for the first prototype, K8854. When taxiing and eventual flight trials began on 23 September 1938, not enough thrust was being produced by the original propeller and, despite a take-off run of almost a mile, the pilot, George Pickering, could not get K8854 into the air. A three-blade propeller was fitted and, after a 30 second run, K8854 did struggle into the air on 29 September. The problem was finally resolved by fitting a four blade prop arranged in a scissor pattern, set 35° apart instead of the usual 90°. Performance was vastly improved but, by the time the aircraft entered production, the Mercury XXX engine was available and was first flown in January 1941. After a host of further modifications because of specification changes, the first production Sea Otter flew in January 1943.

Operational Service

Despite being seen as more likely to be an FAA aircraft, the Sea Otter Mk II first entered service with the RAF's 277 Squadron at Shoreham in November 1943. The Sea Otter also later served with 276, 278, 279, 281, 282 and 292 Squadrons as well as 1347, 1348, 1349, 1350, 1351 and 1352 Flights often serving alongside the type it was meant to replace, the Walrus. RAF service came to an end in October 1945 when 278 Squadron disbanded at Beccles and 281 Squadron disbanded at Ballykelly.

FAA service came even later in the war when the Sea Otter ASR Mk II (Naval) joined 1700 Squadron at Lee-on-Solent in November 1944. With little chance to outshine its famous predecessor, only four FAA squadrons had been re-equipped by the time World War Two came to an end. The type did remain in FAA service until January 1952, during which time it had also served with 700, 712, 716, 721, 723, 728, 733, 740, 742, 744, 771, 772, 778, 781, 790, 799, 810, 1701, 1702 and 1703 Squadrons.

Eight aircraft apiece were also ordered by the RDAF and the Dutch Naval Air Arm. The French colonial service also bought six for operations in French Indochina.

A few Sea Otters also saw service on the civilian register across the globe being converted to carry up to four passengers or freight, or a combination of the two.

Production

In total, 592 Sea Otters were ordered but only 292 were actually built. Two prototypes, K8854 and K8855, ordered to specification 5/36 and contract 493798/36 as the Type 309 followed by six production orders. Three of these orders were to be sub-contracted to Saunders-Roe and two more to Blackburn. Only one Saunders-Roe contract for 250 aircraft was fully completed and a second was part completed before cancellation.

Technical data – Sea Otter	
ENGINE	One 965hp Bristol Mercury XXX
WINGSPAN	46ft
LENGTH	39ft 10¾in
HEIGHT (on ground)	15ft 1½in
WING AREA	610 sq ft
EMPTY WEIGHT	6,805lb
LOADED WEIGHT	10,000lb
MAX SPEED	163mph at 4,500ft
ALIGHTING SPEED (without power)	65mph
CLIMB RATE	870ft/min, 5,000ft in 7 min
CEILING	17,000ft
RANGE (normal)	690 miles
RANGE (maximum)	920 miles with overload tank

Work on the Sea Otter proceeded slowly at first because of Supermarine's commitments to Spitfire and, ironically, Walrus production. Further protractions did not see the type enter service until late 1943, but unlike many other service types it continued into the post-war era and was not retired by the FAA until 1952. (*Aeroplane*)

The High-Speed Spitfire

Development

Despite the clouds of war gathering over Europe, the thought of breaking the World Air Speed Record had been burning away since Flt Lt G H Stainforth's S.6B record was breached by Francesco Agello in the MC.72 on 10 April 1933. Agello beat his own record again on 23 October 1934 in the same aircraft, raising the bar to 440.5mph. This was still the speed to beat in 1939.

Design

The aircraft selected for the challenge was the 48th Spitfire Mk I off the production line, K9834. With Air Ministry backing, the Spitfire was redesignated as the Type 323 under contract 817241/38 for the AMDP (Air Member for Development and Production). The fighter was heavily modified, having its wing span reduced to 33ft 8in and the cockpit canopy lowered, streamlined and extended forward. The riveting was also smoothed down so they were flush to the skin, and the entire aircraft was finished in high-gloss paint.

Power was provided by a 2,160hp Rolls-Royce Merlin 3M, fitted with a four-blade, fixed-pitch propeller. As a result of the new engine, a larger radiator and oil cooler was also fitted. The finishing touch was a slim tail skid rather than the standard tail wheel and, by early November 1938, this standard Mk I was rolled out as the 'High Speed Spitfire'.

Operational service

Now registered for 'Class B' racing and displaying the registration N-17, the Spitfire was flown by 'Mutt' Summers on 11 November 1938. Supermarine was confident that N-17 could breach Agello's record but, frustratingly, before an attempt was made, the record was broken by the Germans on 30 March 1939. Hans Dieterle, flying an He100V8 shattered the record with a speed of 463.919mph only to be pipped on 26 April by Fritz Wendel in a Me209V1, who raised the record to 469.22mph, which stood until the Meteor F.4s broke it again in November 1945.

This left the High Speed Spitfire way behind and all work trying to improve the performance of the aircraft was stopped. N-17 did teach engineers a huge amount about high speed flight, especially with regard to engine cooling. Various propellers were also experimented with, including a controllable pitch de Havilland three-blade. During this time, the aircraft was used as a sales tool, appearing at the Paris Salon in July 1939.

The Spitfire was returned to normal RAF duties as K9834, and it was reverted to a Mk I configuration to serve with the PDU (Photographic Development Unit) at Heston. It was then converted to a PR Mk I and then a PR Mk III before joining 1 PRU (Photographic Reconnaissance Unit) at Benson on 24 November 1940.

A landing accident at Benson in August 1942 saw K9834 spending a few weeks with Heston Aircraft being repaired before returning back to 1 PRU in early September. The aircraft then spent the remainder of its entire service operating from Benson without mishap until it was SOC on 21 August 1946.

Technical data – Spitfire F Mk I K9834	
ENGINE	One 2,160hp Rolls-Royce Merlin 3M
WINGSPAN	33ft 8in
LENGTH	29ft 11in
MAX SPEED	420mph (projected)

Looking every inch a world beater, ex-Spitfire Mk I K9834 on display following its transformation into the High Speed Spitfire N-17. (Via Martyn Chorlton)

Type 322 S.24/37 'Dumbo'

Development

As early as 1937, a new requirement for ship-borne torpedo dive-bomber reconnaissance to replace the Albacore was issued, despite the Fairey machine not flying until December 1938.

Following the publication of Specification S.24/37, tenders from seven different manufacturers were received, but only Supermarine and Fairey were awarded contracts for a pair of prototypes apiece. Supermarine was already preoccupied with producing the Spitfire, so Fairey could focus more time on its entry, which eventually entered service as the Barracuda. While the Supermarine design, designated Type 322 did not enter service, it incorporated several interesting and advanced features including a variable-incidence wing.

Design

S.24/37 called for a very robust monoplane that could stand the rigors of deck landings and take-offs with better performance than the Albacore, especially maximum speed and range. Other exacting criteria included an all-up not to exceed 10,500lb, able to perform a dive-bombing angle of 70° to the horizontal and its dimensions would be restricted by the size of the current Royal Navy's lifts.

Power was to be provided by a British air-cooled engine driving a variable-pitch propeller. Supermarine chose the 24-cylinder Rolls-Royce Exe engine but by 1938 it had been cancelled so the company could, wisely, concentrate on developing the Merlin. It was the Merlin 30 which, although water-cooled was available in abundance by the time the Type 322 was nearing completion.

The aircraft was mainly built of wood because of the shortage of light alloys at the time. Aft of the firewall, the Type 322 was made of diagonal-grain plywood glued to the main structure, made up of spruce longerons and wooden frames in a similar style to the S.4.

The composite wing was made in three sections with a centre and a pair of outer planes. Naval requirements meant that, when the wings were folded, the main spar flanges were unbroken, thanks to a folding joint located on a raked spar. The main spar was fitted out with duralumin flanges and webs and the rear spar and ribs were made of wood. The first prototype, R1810, had its wing covered in diagonal ply while the second, R1815, was covered in Alclad sheet that increased torsional rigidity.

Variable incidence would give the pilot superb visibility, which was particularly useful on a big tail dragger operating from a carrier. The wing could be moved through two degrees with the flaps up and 16° when the flaps were fully lowered. The lift coefficient was twice the average at 3.9 (the Lysander was only 2.38) and a stalling speed of around 58mph could be achieved.

Service

The first prototype, Type 322 R1810, nicknamed 'Dumbo' because of its elephant-like shape, first flew on 6 February 1943. The second aircraft, R1815, powered by a Merlin 32, first flew not long after and following Supermarine's own trials, R1810 was delivered to the RAE in November 1944. Incidentally, Fairey's own design was equally as challenging to meet S.24/37 and the Barracuda did not enter service until 1943, five years after the specification was issued.

Production

Two aircraft, R1810 and R1815, were ordered 17 May 1939 under contract 976687/39.

Technical data – Type 322	
ENGINE	(R1810) One 1,300hp Rolls-Royce Merlin 30. (R1815) One 1,645hp Merlin 32
WINGSPAN	50ft
LENGTH	40ft
HEIGHT	14ft 2in
WING AREA	319½ sq ft
EMPTY WEIGHT	9,175lb
LOADED WEIGHT	12,000lb
MAX SPEED	279mph at 4,000ft
STALLING SPEED	58mph
CLIMB RATE	870 ft/min. 5,000ft in 7 min
CEILING	17,000ft
RANGE (maximum)	825 miles at 160mph at 2,000ft with 30 gal reserve tank
ARMAMENT	One 18in Mk XII 1,500lb torpedo or six 250lb or six 500lb bombs. One .303in Browning machine-gun and one .303in Vickers K or Browning machine-gun in the rear cockpit

The second prototype Type 322 'Dumbo' R1815, displaying the wing's full-span slats and flaps in the high-lift position. (Via Martyn Chorlton)

The Type 322 was certainly not a good-looking aircraft, but neither was the aircraft chosen for Specification S.24/37, the Barracuda. This is R1810 demonstrating the wings folded position, which, like the variable incidence idea, was a piece of engineering excellence. (*Aeroplane*)

Spitfire Mk IIA, Mk IIB & Mk IIC (ASR.II)

Development

In June 1939, Spitfire Mk I K9788 was sent to Rolls-Royce at Hucknall to be fitted with a 1,150hp Merlin XII (RM3S) engine to improve on the rate of climb and ceiling. Following successful trials at Martlesham Heath, the Spitfire Mk II was born, which was destined to be exclusively built at the brand new Nuffield shadow factory at Castle Bromwich.

Design

On the surface, the Mk II looked little different from the Mk I and the only indication of the presence of a different engine was a small blister on the starboard engine for access to a Coffman 'shotgun' type starter. The Merlin XII was the first of its breed to use a 70/30 water to Glycol coolant mix rather than all Glycol. This was not an insignificant modification as Glycol was an expensive and rare commodity. The other obvious physical change was the propeller, which was a Rotol wide-bladed design measuring 10ft 9in in diameter. A shortage of these saw the reintroduction of the de Havilland propeller for some of the later production Mk IIs.

Three versions of the latest Spitfire were produced; the Mk IIA fitted with eight .303in machine-guns, the Mk IIB with four .303in machine-guns plus a pair of 20mm Hispano cannons and finally the lesser known Mk IIC. The latter was the designation given to 50 Mk IIs that were converted for ASR operations to become the Type 375. The conversion included a Merlin XX engine, the ability to carry a dinghy and survival gear stowed in the parachute flare chutes. The aircraft was reclassified in 1942 to the ASR.II because of the confusion caused by the Type C universal wing.

Performance was only marginally better than the Mk I, improving top speed by about 7mph below 17,000ft, although the rate of climb was improved. The increased weight reduced the potential improvement but the Mk II's strength was its fighting capability because the flexibility of the weapons it could carry.

Several Mk IIs were modified to carry long-range 40 gallon fuel tanks under the port wing in 1941. While the range was increased, so was drag and this saw the performance and manoeuvrability dramatically reduced. This did not stop several units from using them on some of the early *Circus* bomber escort operations over Northern France.

Operational service

There were several production delays with the Mk II and it was not until June 1940 that the first were delivered. The Spitfire Mk IIA entered service with 152 Squadron in July 1940 and its first operational sortie was flown by 611 Squadron at Duxford on 31 August 1940. Because of the long-range tank option, the Mk II flew the first Fighter Command sweeps over Europe, the first being carried out by 66 Squadron from Biggin Hill on 20 December 1940.

The following RAF units operated the Mk II, 19, 41, 54, 64, 65, 66, 71, 72, 74, 91, 111, 118, 121, 122, 123, 124, 129, 130, 131, 132, 133, 134, 145, 152, 154, 222, 234, 266, 276, 277, 278, 302, 303, 306, 308, 310, 312, 313, 315, 316, 331, 340, 350, 401, 403, 411, 412, 416, 417, 452, 457, 485, 501, 504, 602, 603, 609, 610, 611 and 616. Only one FAA unit, 759 Squadron flew the Mk II.

Production

The original order was for 1,000 Mk IIs ordered under contract B.981687/39/CB/23(c) on 12 April 1939 at Castle Bromwich as Mk IIA. In total, 972 were actually built in the serial range P7280 to P8799.

Technical data – Spitfire Mk II	
ENGINE	One 1,150hp Rolls-Royce Merlin RM XII and a small number fitted with the Merlin 45 and III
WINGSPAN	36ft 10in
LENGTH	29ft 11in
HEIGHT (prop vertical, tail down)	11ft 5in
WING AREA	242 sq ft
TARE WEIGHT	4,783lb
TAKE-OFF WEIGHT	6,275lb
MAX SPEED (Merlin X)	370mph at rated altitude
CLIMB	5,000ft in 1 min 42 secs
CLIMB RATE (initial)	2,600ft/min
CEILING	32,800ft
ARMAMENT	A wing (Mk II Star guns) or F Mk IIB 2 x 20mm Hispano cannon 60rpg and 4 x .303in Browning machine guns 300rpg (B Wing)

Confusion reigned for many years over this Spitfire, which wears the codes of 92 Squadron (who never operated the Mk II) but is on the strength of 616 Squadron. The aircraft, Mk IIA P7753, is pictured at Tangmere in early 1941. It was damaged by return fire from a Ju88 off Littlehampton on 5 May 1941 and abandoned by its pilot, Flt Lt L H Casson. (Via Martyn Chorlton)

Ground crew of 276 Squadron at Warmwell loading dinghies into ASR. IIC P8131 flown by Flt Lt N Berryman. The Spitfire served with the squadron from April 1943 to February 1945 followed by further service with 1 AGS and 10 AGS before being SOC on 18 June 1945. (Via Martyn Chorlton)

Spitfire Mk III

Development

Rather than becoming the next mass-produced example of the Spitfire, the Mk III, of which only two were built, served to give Supermarine an opportunity to see how far they had come since 1936 and to embody all that experience into the next stage of development. It was an aircraft that attempted to improve upon the basic design and, in many respects, achieved it. However, the Mk III was destined to benefit future marks.

Design

By 1940, engine development was accelerating and the introduction of 1,240hp Merlin XX gave Supermarine another opportunity to improve its Spitfire. The engine was installed in N3297 (originally built as a Mk I at Southampton under contract 527113/36), the first of two Mk IIIs which was intended as an aircraft that would embody all service experience gained from the first two marks.

Other features included clipped wings, reducing the span to 30ft 6in and introducing the Type C universal armament wing that was used on many later variants. A internal laminated bullet-proof windscreen was introduced and inverted, making the forward part of windscreen drag free. The undercarriage was made stronger, fitted with wheel cover flaps and, a retractable tail wheel was also fitted to reduce drag still further. The undercarriage was also raked forward by two inches to improve ground stability which had always been a problem with the Spitfire.

Incredibly, the total time it had taken to create this host of modification, was nearly 90,000 man-hours. While the Mk III never blossomed, the labour-intensive improved features were nearly all incorporated into later marks.

Service

The first Mk III prototype, N3297, first flew on 16 March 1940 followed by the second, W3237 (built as a Mk V), on 4 June 1941. Both aircraft served as very useful development aircraft. N3297 was later converted into the prototype Mk IX. W3237 carried out extended wing tip and four position flap trials with the A&AEE at Boscombe Down and later with the FAA at Worthy Down.

One of the contributory factors to the decision not to expand production of the Mk III, (although a large order was received and later cancelled) was the lack of Merlin XX engines available. Instead, the engine was diverted to the Hurricane Mk II and Defiant Mk II and, by the time availability had improved, Supermarine were already working on the Spitfire Mk V.

Production

Two aircraft built, N3297 and W3237, were built as Type 330 (later Type 348) Mk III to contract B23634/39.

Technical data – Spitfire Mk III	
ENGINE	One 1,240hp Rolls-Royce Merlin RM 3SM XX
WINGSPAN	32ft 7in
LENGTH	30ft 4in
WING AREA	220 sq ft
MAX SPEED (Merlin X)	340mph at 5,000ft, 360mph at 10,000ft, 400mph at 20,000ft
CLIMB	15,000ft in 4.5 min, 20,000ft in 6.4 min
CEILING (service)	38,000ft
ARMAMENT	(proposed); Four 20mm Hispano cannon (inboard) and four .303in Colt Browning machine-guns (outboard)

Above: The first of two Spitfires converted to Mk III standard was N3297. The clipped wing, smoother windscreen and unpainted panel for the retractable tail-wheel can be clearly seen. (Via Martyn Chorlton)

Right: A very rare photograph of the second Mk III converted ex-Mk V W3237. Note the retractable tailwheel doors and the wheel cover flaps on the main undercarriage. This idea was first seen with the prototype Hurricane and then dispensed with as no noticeable aerodynamic benefit was achieved. (Via Martyn Chorlton)

Spitfire Mk VA, VB & VC

Development

By far the most prolific of Spitfires produced was the Mk V, which had no less than six variants in both high and low altitude roles. The Mk V also introduced the Merlin 45 series of engines, which was first fitted into ex-PR Mk III X4334 at Hucknall under the supervision of Ray Dorey. Within the space of three years, nearly 6,500 Mk Vs had been built, the majority of them at Castle Bromwich.

Design

The original Mk V was little more than a Mk I with a Merlin 45, which was a variant of Merlin XX. The second stage of the supercharger was removed and a new single stage one was redesigned giving the power plant 1,440hp.

The first variant, the Mk VA, was introduced with eight .303in machine guns followed by the Mk VB with two 20mm cannons and four .303in machine guns and by the Mk VC fitted with a universal wing as tested on the Spitfire Mk III.

All of the variants had additional armoured protection and extra heating for the gun bays for high-altitude operations. The fuel supply was also improved by combining a more efficient carburettor fitted to the Merlin engine and fuel tanks which pressurised above 25,000ft. A tropical filter was fitted for operations in the Middle East and jettisonable fuel tanks could also be fitted.

Operational service

The RAF received its first Spitfire Mk Vs in February 1941. 92 Squadron at Biggin Hill was the first recipient. Within a short space of time, the mark became the backbone of Fighter Command operations, featuring prominently in *Rhubarb* and *Circus* operations during 1941 and 1942 over Northern Europe.

The Mk VB became the first Spitfire to serve overseas when 15 of them arrived in Malta on 7 March 1942. By August 1942, there were three squadrons in the Western Desert and, from February 1942, the Mk V also introduced the Spitfire to the Pacific theatre when 54 Squadron took delivery during the defence of Darwin, Australia. From October 1943, the Mk V also appeared in Burmese skies with 136, 607 and 615 Squadrons.

The following RAF squadrons operated the Mk V; 16, 19, 26, 32, 33, 41, 54, 63, 64, 65, 66, 71, 72, 73, 74, 80, 81, 87, 91, 92, 93, 94, 111, 118, 121, 122, 123, 124, 126, 127, 129, 130, 131, 132, 133, 134, 136, 145, 152, 154, 164, 165, 167, 184, 185, 186, 208, 213, 222, 225, 229, 232, 234, 237, 238, 241, 242, 243, 249, 253, 257, 266, 269, 274, 275, 276, 277, 278, 287, 288, 290, 302, 303, 306, 308, 310, 312, 313, 315, 316, 317, 318, 322, 326, 327, 328, 329, 331, 332, 335, 336, 340, 341, 345, 349, 350, 352, 401, 402, 403, 411, 412, 416, 417, 421, 441, 442, 443, 451, 452, 453, 457, 485, 501, 504, 520, 521, 527, 567, 577, 595, 601, 602, 603, 607, 609, 610, 611, 615, 616, 631, 691, 695 and 1435 Squadrons.

The following FAA squadrons also operated all three marks; (VA) 736, 748, 759, 761, 794, 801, 809, 879, 884, 885 and 887; (VB) 719, 748, 759, 761, 768, 770, 778, 787, 790, 791, 794, 798, 801, 808, 879, 880, 884, 885, 886, 894, 897, 899; and (VC) 775 Squadron.

Production

In total, 6,487 Mk VA, VB and VC types were built between 1940 and 1943 in 17 production batches by Supermarine Aviation (Vickers), Vickers-Armstrongs and Westland Aircraft Ltd. The most prolific of the Mk Vs built was the Mk VC, of which 2,482 were made.

Technical data – Spitfire MK VA, VB AND VC	
ENGINE	One 1,440hp Rolls-Royce Merlin 45
WINGSPAN	32ft 2in
LENGTH	29ft 11in
HEIGHT (prop vertical, tail down)	11ft 5½in
WING AREA	231 sq ft
TARE WEIGHT	5,050lb
LOADED WEIGHT	6,650lb
MAX SPEED	(VA) 357mph at 6,000ft, 375mph at 20,800ft
CLIMB	(VA) 20,000ft in 5.6 min
RATE OF CLIMB (initial)	4,750 ft/min
RANGE	470 miles at cruising speed of 272mph
CEILING (service)	35,500ft
ARMAMENT	(VA) Eight .303 machine guns. (VB) Four .303in machine-guns, two 20mm Hispano cannon. (VC) Capable of mounting 'A' or 'B' armament or four 20mm Hispano cannon

Above: Beautiful study of Spitfire LF Mk VB BL479 of 316 'City of Warsaw' Squadron, during a sortie from Hutton Cranswick, North Yorkshire in October 1942. (Charles E. Brown via Martyn Chorlton)

Right: A Merlin 45-powered Spitfire Mk VA sporting a tropical air intake filter in appropriate weather in January 1942. (Via Martyn Chorlton)

Spitfire F Mk IV

Development

The idea of powering a Spitfire by a Rolls-Royce Griffon engined first showed itself in a brochure published by the Supermarine design staff on 4 December 1939. Chief Designer Joe Smith was rightly optimistic of the aircraft's potential performance, confidently predicting that 423mph at 18,500ft could be achieved.

The Griffon machine would not appear as quickly as Supermarine hoped for because of development problems with the new engine but following successful trials with the Spitfire F Mk IV, full production finally beckoned in 1942.

Design

The Type 337 Spitfire F Mk IV was powered by a single-stage supercharged 1,725hp Griffin IIB engine driving a Rotol 10ft 5in propeller. A larger radiator and oil cooler were fitted and, to cope with the extra weight of the engine, stronger main longerons were fitted. The Griffon had a lower thrust-line than the Merlin and as a result the shape of engine cowling was completely different. Blisters were also needed to clear the cylinder heads and the magneto. The lower cowling lost the 'puffed-out' look as well, the Griffon engine giving the F Mk IV a much shallower curve up towards the spinner.

The general airframe, apart from the differences mentioned, was very similar to the Mk III including a C Type wing and a retractable tail wheel.

Service

The first of two Type 337 F Mk IV prototypes, DP845 was first flown from Worthy Down by Jeffrey Quill on 27 November 1941. Quill was quite taken by the new fighter describing as follows:

> ...[T]here was somewhat less ground clearance, resulting in a slight reduction in propeller diameter. The power available for take-off was much greater, and the engine RPM was lower than in the Merlin. All this meant that the throttle needed to be handled judiciously on take-off but, once in the air, the aeroplane had a great feeling of power about it. It seemed to be the airborne equivalent of a very powerful sports car and was great fun to fly. Changes of trim with changes of power were much more in evidence, both directionally and longitudinally, and the aeroplane sheared about a bit during tight manoeuvres and simulated dog-fights. I realised at once that we should have to correct its directional characteristics and probably its longitudinal stability also, both of which in due time we achieved. Indeed, DP485 eventually went through many phases of development throughout and I, and others, flew in it a great deal; it became one of our favourite aeroplanes.

To avoid confusion with the new PR Mk IV, the aircraft was redesignated as the Mk XX and then again as the Mk XII which did enter limited production. The second F Mk IV, DP851 first flew in December 1941 and was later converted into the prototype F.21.

Production

Two Mk IV prototypes, DP845 and DP851, were ordered with Supermarine on 26 May 1941, to specification F4/41. Main production order for 750 aircraft (ER206 to ES369) was placed on 23 August 1941 under contract 981687/39/C.23(c) but all were built as MK VB and Mk VC instead.

Technical data – Spitfire F Mk IV	
ENGINE	One 1,445hp Rolls-Royce Griffon RG 2SM IIB
WING AREA	242 sq ft
TARE WEIGHT	5,985lb
MAX SPEED	374mph at 5,000ft, 433mph at 23,500ft, 388mph at 25,000ft
CLIMB	15,000ft in 4.5 min, 20,000ft in 6.6 min
CEILING (service)	46,300ft
CEILING (operational)	43,500ft
ARMAMENT	Up to six 20mm Hispano cannon

The prototype Spitfire F Mk IV enjoyed a lengthy flying career and was involved in a host of trials with various Griffon engines before being SOC in 1946. (Via Martyn Chorlton)

Seafire Mk IB

Development

The Admiralty had been trying to obtain its own version of the Spitfire or 'Sea Spitfire' for operations from aircraft carriers since 1940. With the Battle of Britain raging, the country needed every fighter it could get its hands on and the request was unsurprisingly denied. By 1941, the dust was settling and Britain, now partly relieved by the thought that Hitler was not about to invade, took the Navy's request more seriously. Several Spitfire Mk Is and 49 Mk VBs were diverted to the FAA and two of the latter batch, AD205 and AD371, were fitted with arrestor hooks and catapult spools at Worthy Down.

Design

Following the successful 'navalised' conversion of the two Mk VBs, the remainder was converted by Air Training Service Ltd at Hamble, redesignated as the 'hooked' Spitfire.

This preliminary batch of aircraft was intended to be used by the Royal Navy to gain experience of operating the type from aircraft carriers, clearly not a role that R J Mitchell had intended the fighter for.

Structural changes included making the lower rear fuselage incorporate an A-frame type arrestor hook and beefing up the lower longerons. It was not long before the fuselage was found to be too weak for carrier operations and reinforcing strips were added around hatch openings and all of the fuselage longerons. None of this first batch was fitted with catapult spools.

The aircraft, first called the Seafire Mk IB, was BL676, originally built as an Mk VB, the aircraft was delivered to Hamble on 10 January 1942. The fighter was fitted with catapult spools, slinging points, a tropical filter, a 30-gallon auxiliary/slipper fuel tank and was strengthened at various points along the fuselage. BL676, which was re-serialled as MB328, first flew from Worthy Down on 23 March 1942.

Operational service

Only two front line operational units were 'fully' equipped with the Seafire Mk IB; firstly 801 Squadron on board HMS *Furious* from October 1942 to September 1944. 842 Squadron followed in July 1943, embarking on HMS *Fencer* but these were withdrawn by March 1944.

The following units also had at least one Seafire Mk IB on strength, 700, 708, 715, 719, 731, 736, 748, 759, 760 (Reserve) 761, 768, 778, 779, 781, 787, 787Y, 790, 798, 801, 807, 809, 816, 842, 879, 885, 887, 894 and 897 Squadrons. The type was also used by No.1 and 2 Naval Fighter Schools at Yeovilton and Henstridge, respectively, the School of Naval Warfare at St Merryn and RNAS Lee-on-Solent and Stretton.

Production

The first production order was for 48 Type 340 Mk IB (MB328 to MB375) conversions with tropical filters, from Spitfire F Mk VB by Air Service Training (AST) Ltd, Hamble.

Second production was 138 Mk IB (NX879-PA129) conversions of Spitfire Mk VB originally ordered 25 March 1942 from AST Ltd, Hamble, under contract No.2259. PA100-PA129 later transferred to Phillips & Powis for completion at South Marston.

Technical data – Seafire Mk IB	
ENGINE	One 1,470hp Rolls-Royce Merlin 45 or 1,415hp Merlin 46
WINGSPAN	36ft 10in
LENGTH	30ft 2½in
HEIGHT	11ft 5½in
WING AREA	231 sq ft
EMPTY WEIGHT	5,100lb
LOADED WEIGHT	6,700lb
MAX SPEED	365mph at 16,000ft
RANGE	492 miles
CEILING (service)	36,400ft
ARMAMENT	Four .303in machine-guns and two 20mm Hispano cannon

Spitfire Mk IBs of 736 Squadron (School of Air Combat), which was the equivalent to the RAF's Fighter Leaders School. The squadron operated the type at Yeovilton and St Merryn from May 1943 through to August 1944. (*Aeroplane*)

Spitfire HF Mk VI

Development

The Spitfire Mk VI came about because of the perceived threat of enemy bombers attacking Britain at very high altitude. The appearance of the Junkers Ju 86P in particular, which could easily operate above 40,000ft, prompted the rapid development of a Spitfire that could reach and fight at the same altitude.

Design

The HF Mk VI was based on the Mk VB but differed in the following areas. The cockpit was pressurised with a differential of 2 psi, which meant that when the aircraft was flying at 40,000ft, the pilot was experiencing the same effects of the aircraft being at 30,000ft. Pressurisation was achieved by a pressure –tight forward and rear cockpit bulkheads, structural joints were sealed and rubber sealing grommets/glands were installed for the piping and control cables. The development of the high-altitude Wellington Mk V and Mk VI had contributed enormously to this design.

The side opening cockpit door was also removed and skinned over and the canopy was replaced with a sliding one. When the pilot was inside, the canopy was locked down by four toggles and sealed by an inflatable rubber tube. If the pilot needed to get out in a hurry, the canopy could be jettisoned.

Power was provided by a Merlin 47, which was fitted with a Marshall blower that provided the pressurisation. A four-blade Rotol propeller was fitted for better efficiency at altitude and increased performance.

The wings were standard Type Bs but the wing tips were tapered and extended to 40ft 2in to improve the air flow.

Operational service

The Spitfire HF Mk VI first entered service with 616 Squadron in April 1942, by which time the thought of hundreds of bombers flying at high altitude unmolested and disappeared. The type was then operated at lower altitude instead where it was outperformed by unmodified Spitfires. Only 124 and 616 Squadron were fully equipped with the Mk IV while the following units did have a few on strength: 66, 118, 129, 132, 234, 310, 313, 504, 519, 602, and 680 Squadrons.

Production

Two prototypes were converted, R7120 and X4942, the latter flying as Mk VI first in June 1941. One hundred aircraft, according to Supermarine records, were produced including 14 that were converted from Mk VB, VC, PR Mk VI and PR Mk IV during 1941 and 1942. BR159 to BS472 were all built as the HF VI (PC) with a Merlin 47 engine.

Technical data – Spitfire HF Mk VI	
ENGINE	One 1,415hp Rolls-Royce Merlin 47
WINGSPAN	40ft 2in
WING AREA	248.5 sq ft
TARE WEIGHT	5,227lb
TAKE-OFF WEIGHT	6,797lb
MAX SPEED	264mph at 40,000ft, 364mph at 21,500ft and 300mph at 12,000ft
CLIMB	39,000ft in 34.5 mins, 20,000ft in 8¾ mins
CLIMB RATE (max)	1,310ft/min at 30,000ft
RANGE	475 miles at 150mph
CEILING (service)	40,000ft
ARMAMENT	Two 20mm Hispano cannon

The high-altitude Spitfire Mk VI with extended wingtips, a pressurised cabin fitted with a Merlin 47 engine driving a four-blade propeller. (Via Martyn Chorlton)

Seafire L/F/FR.IIC & LR.IIC

Development

The Mk IIC was the first purpose built Seafire, rather than a conversion of a Spitfire, which first entered service with the FAA in July 1942 at the same time as the Mk IB. The prototype was still a converted Spitfire Mk VC and, at first, its performance was no better than the Seafire Mk IB but it was stronger, and more powerful, incorporating lessons learned from earlier carrier operations.

Design

The Seafire IIC, which took advantage of the refinements of the Spitfire Mk VC over the Mk VB, was fitted with catapult spool, a strong fuselage, a reinforced undercarriage, and the prototype, AD371, was fitted with a Merlin 32 engine driving a Rotol four-blade propeller. Production aircraft would be built with the Merlin 45 and 46 engines.

Three sub-variants were built, the F.IIC, the FR.IIC, both powered by the Merlin 45 and 46 and the L.IIC fitted with a Merlin 32 all driving a 10ft 9in four-blade propeller. The 45/46 powered machines had a top speed that was 15mph less than the Seafire Mk IB, although performance at altitude was much better. However, the majority of naval interceptions took place at low level and this was where the Merlin 32 was at its best. Top speed at sea level rose to 316mph and at 6,000ft it was 335mph while take-off runs were reduced and the rate of climb from low altitude increased as well. The Merlin 32 improved the mark so much the engine was transferred from Barracuda Mk II production to cater for the Seafire IIC.

The Type C wing allowed for a pair of 20mm Hispano cannon and four .303in machines, giving the naval fighter quite a punch; a single 250lb could also be carried.

The IIC also introduced RATOG (Rocket Assisted Take Off Gear), which was first trialled on MB141/G and MB125 in February 1943 and would later become the standard method of taking off from a carrier.

Operational service

After its first flight in February 1942, AD371 was delivered to RAE Farnborough for trials and then on to 778 Squadron at Arbroath. The first production aircraft, MA971, was delivered to the Royal Navy on 2 June 1942 and by July was serving at RNAS Lee-on-Solent. The mark went on to see widespread operational use with 700, 708, 718, 719, 728, 731, 736, 748, 757, 759, 761, 768, 770, 775, 776, 778, 787, 787Y, 790, 798, 799, 801, 807, 808, 809, 816, 833, 834, 842, 879, 880, 884, 885, 886, 887, 889, 894, 895, 897 and 899 Squadrons.

Because of its inability to fold its wings, the type was phased out quite quickly in favour of the Seafire F.III, although several LR.IICs served on into the post-war period.

Production

In total, 372 Seafire Mk IIs were built in three production batches during 1942 and 1943 by Supermarine (Vickers) Ltd and Westland Aircraft Ltd: 262 were built by Supermarine and 110 by Westland.

Technical data – Spitfire F.IIC	
ENGINE	(FR/L/LR/PR.IIC) One 1,645hp Rolls-Royce Merlin 32. (F.IIC) One 1,470/1,415hp Merlin 45/46
WINGSPAN	36ft 10in
LENGTH	30ft 2½in
HEIGHT (prop vertical, tail down)	11ft 2½in
WING AREA	242 sq ft
TARE WEIGHT	5,215lb
LOADED WEIGHT	6,665lb
MAX SPEED	(L.IIC) 333mph at 5,000ft. (LR.IIC) 365mph at 16,000ft
CLIMB	20,000ft in 5.7 min
RATE OF CLIMB (initial)	2,950 ft/min
RANGE	493 miles at cruising speed of 188mph
CEILING (service)	32,000ft
ARMAMENT	(F.IIC) Four .303in machine-guns and two 20mm Hispano cannon. One 250lb bomb on the centreline
CAMERA	(PR later FR & LR.IIC) One F.24 (8 or 14in focal length) and one F.24 (5, 8, 14 or 20in focal length in the vertical)

Seafire Mk IIC MB146 of 885 Squadron on HMS *Formidable* in late 1942. The fighter joined the carrier in October 1942, in time to see action during Operation *Torch*, the allied invasion of North Africa. The fighter was destined to only last two months before being written off in a landing accident on 26 November 1942. (*Aeroplane*)

Spitfire PR Mk IV, VI & VII

Development

From November 1939, converted Spitfires were flying photographic reconnaissance missions from airfields in France and continued to do so from airfields in Britain until the war's end. Early aircraft were converted Mk Is, being redesignated as the PR Mk I with three separate sub-variants. Only limited numbers were converted and it was not until the arrival of the PR MK IV, VI and VII, all based on the Spitfire Mk V, that specialist variants were produced in numbers.

The PR Mk IV (Type D)
The first of the dedicated variants and the one produced in greater numbers was the PR MK IV, which entered service in October 1940. The PR Mk IV had the longest range of any of the early PR Spitfires. It could carry 114 gallons of fuel in its D type wings, giving it a range of 2000 miles – in one of its first missions, a PR Mk IV reached Stettin, in the Baltic! It was known as the 'bowser' because of the amount of fuel she could carry. The PR Mk IV could carry a wide variety of cameras, each given a letter code.

The PR Mk VI (Type F)
The PR Mk VI was an interim design produced to fill a gap before the appearance of the PR Mk IV. It was created by adding two 30-gallon fuel tanks below the wings as well as the extra fuselage tank, giving it an endurance of four and a half hours, which allowed it to reach Berlin. The first flight to the German capital was made on 14 March 1941. The first of 15 PR Mk VIs appeared in March 1940, seven months before the Mk IV.

The PR Mk VII
One danger of using the low level oblique camera was that it put the PR Spitfire back in the range of German fighters. One response was to produce an armed PR Spitfire. The PR Mk VII carried the standard eight machine guns of the Mk IA, combined with the extra fuselage fuel tank of the PR versions.

Operational service

The three marks served with the following RAF squadrons: (IV) 69,140, 540, 541, 542, 543, 544, 680, 681 and 683; (VI) 66, 118,124, 129, 132, 140; (VII) 234, 310, 313, 504, 602, 616 and 680.

Production

Approximately 384 Spitfire PR Mk IV, VI and VIIs were built. This is an estimate as many airframes were converted into different marks on more than one occasion. The PR Mk IV Type D was produced in greater numbers than any other of its breed with 326 built/converted while only 15 PR VI Type Fs and 43 aircraft were converted into the PR Mk VII Type G.

Technical data – Spitfire PR Mk IV, VI and VII	
ENGINE	One 1,100hp Rolls-Royce Merlin 45 or 46
WING AREA	242 sq ft
TARE WEIGHT	(IV) 4,953lb (VII) 4,985lb
TAKE-OFF WEIGHT	(IV) 7,148lb (VII) 6,584lb
ARMAMENT	(VII) Eight .303in machine guns
CAMERAS	(IV and VI) 'W' installation – 2 x F.8 20in split vertical fanned, between fuselage frames 13 and 15 inclined 10° to the vertical and 20° to each other. Hot air heating. 'X' installation – F.24 14in split vertical fanned and 1 x F.24 8in or 14in oblique mounted as 'W' with oblique over front F.24. Inclined at 8½° to the vertical and 17° to each other. Electric heating. 'Y' fixed installation – 1 x F.52 36in vertical used for bomb damage assessment. Mounted between frames 13 and 14. Hot air heating. (VII) 'G' installation – 1 x F.24 5 or 8in vertical (front) and 1 x F.24 8 or 14in vertical (rear) between frames 13 and 14 and 1 x F.24 8in or 14in oblique mounted above front camera. Electric heating.

Long-serving X4492 was originally built as PR Mk III, then a PR Mk IV as pictured here. It was then converted again, this time to a PR Mk VII before becoming the prototype F Mk VI. A classic example of how the production figures can never be totally accurate. (Via Martyn Chorlton)

Spitfire floatplanes

Development
The original idea to fit floats to a Spitfire was prompted by the German invasion of Norway and the need for a fighter which could operate from the country's many Fjords. However, by the time the aircraft was ready, the campaign was over and the project suspended until the idea was raised again for use in the Pacific and the Mediterranean.

Design
The first of five floatplane conversions was carried out at Woolston to Spitfire Mk I R6722, which was nicknamed the 'Narvik Nightmare'. Despite promising results from tank tests at Farnborough, the nickname gives us an idea of how the aircraft performed after being fitted with a pair of Blackburn Roc floats and a ventral fin. Flotation trials were described as 'unsatisfactory' and the idea was shelved. R6722 was later converted back to a landplane and transferred to 54 Squadron.

In 1942, following Japan's entry into World War Two, the idea was revived again. This time, Folland Aircraft carried out the conversion of Mk VB W3760, which included fitting a pair of 25ft 7in long floats, mounted on faired cantilever struts fixed to the mainplanes. Power was provided by a Merlin 45 fitted with an 11ft 3in four-blade propeller, a Vokes filter was also fitted and, like its predecessor, a ventral fin was added under the tail. W3760 also featured several lift hard-points in front and behind the cockpit and the novel fitment of a spin recovery parachute as well.

W3760 was first flown in its seaplane guise by Jeffrey Quill on 12 October 1942 and immediately showed great promise, with a maximum speed of 324mph recorded. Modifications followed, including replacing the Vokes filter with an Aero-Vee type over the carburettor intake, which was extended to stop spray from the floats entering the engine. Armament was retained to Mk VB standard.

Service
Folland converted two more Mk VBs, EP751 and EP754, both powered by Merlin 45 engines. All three Mk VB floatplanes were then shipped to Egypt in October 1943, where it was hoped that the fighters could be covertly operated against German transport aircraft traversing the Eastern Mediterranean. The plan was to use the floatplanes from bases in the Dodecanese Islands, Greece, but this idea was abandoned when Kos and Leros, both of which were British-held, were overrun by the Germans in November 1943. All three aircraft remained in Egypt with no role to play and, by late 1944, were all SOC.

A fifth and final Spitfire, LF Mk IX MK892 was converted to a floatplane by Folland in March 1944. Powered by a Merlin 61, MK892 was an excellent performer, achieving 377mph, which made it the fastest floatplane of World War Two. Intended for operations in the Pacific Theatre, once again, the idea came to nothing and the idea was finally abandoned for good.

Production/conversions
Five Spitfires were converted to floatplanes between 1940 and 1944, beginning with Mk I R6722, Mk VBs W3760, EP751 and EP754 and Mk IX MJ892.

Technical data – Spitfire Seaplane Mk VA, VB and LF Mk IXB	
ENGINE	(VB) One 1,100hp Rolls-Royce Merlin 45. (IXB) One Merlin 61
TARE WEIGHT	(VB W3760) 5,851lb
ALL-UP WEIGHT	(VB W3760) 7,418lb
TAKE-OFF WEIGHT	(IV) 7,148lb. (VII) 6,584lb
MAX SPEED	(VB) 324mph at 19,500ft
RATE OF CLIMB	(VB) 2,450ft/min at 15,500ft
CEILING	33,400ft
ARMAMENT	(IX) Two 20mm Hispano cannon

Mk IXB MJ892 unintentionally became the fastest floatplane of Second World War when it first flew in April 1944. It was later reconverted back to a landplane, serving until 22 November 1945 when it was SOC. (Via Martyn Chorlton)

Spitfire F Mk VII & HF Mk VII

Development

Intended as an advanced version of the pressurised Mk VI, the Mk VII refined the theory a little further through the addition of more power and pilot-friendly modifications. Supermarine were confident that this mark would be a Mk V replacement, which was originally classed as an interim, while the Mk VII was planned for massed production.

Design

Both the F and HF Mk VII introduced a new breed of engine, the two-speed two-stage Merlin 60 and 70 series, which moved the evolution of the Spitfire to a new level.

The Mk VI's extended wing tips were retained and the retractable tail wheel, developed by the Mk III, was also fitted. The leading edge of each wing was fitted with a small fuel tank for the first time. The new engine gave the Mk VII a longer nose and to counteract this, a larger rudder and trim tab, making the fuselage longer and stronger.

Power for the F Mk VII was either a Merlin 61, rated at 1,300hp at 23,000ft, or a Merlin 64 rated at 1,450hp at 21,000ft. Both engines were fitted with a two stage supercharger for improved performance at high altitude. A new more powerful cooling system was also required and a pair of air scoops, one under each wing was fitted. The HF Mk VII was fitted with a Merlin 71 engine, which was fitted with the innovative Bendix 'anti-g' injection carburettor.

The Mk VI's solution of bolting the pilot into his aircraft was never a popular one but the Mk VII was fitted with a more suitable 'Lobelle' double-glazed sliding cockpit canopy. An advanced version of the Marshall compressor was used for pressurising the cockpit.

Operational service

The Mk VII prototype, AB450, was first flown in June 1942 and by September the first examples entered RAF service with the High Altitude Flight at Northolt. It was not until March 1943 that the type was received by an operational unit, namely 124 Squadron flying from North Weald. Not long after, the unit scored its first Mk VII success when BS142 intercepted a Fw190 over Plymouth and shot it down from 38,000ft. As well as 124 Squadron, the Mk VII was also operated by 118, 131, 154, 313, 518, 519, 611 and 616 Squadrons.

The Mk VII was only marginally more successful than its predecessor and, with the arrival of the Mk IX, was no longer the premier high-altitude Spitfire.

Production

In total, 164 Mk VIIs were produced as a single prototype, AB450, followed by three production batches in the serial ranges, BS121, BS142, BS229, BS253, BS427, EN178-EN512 and MB761-MD190, built between August 1942 and early 1944.

Technical data – Spitfire F Mk VII and HF Mk VII	
ENGINE	(F Mk VII) One 1,565hp Rolls-Royce Merlin 61 or one 1,710hp Merlin 64 (HF Mk VII)One 1,700hp (at 18,000ft) Merlin 71
LENGTH	31ft 3½in
SPAN	40ft 2in
TARE WEIGHT	('Lobelle' hood) 5,947lb (Standard hood) 5,887lb
MAX WEIGHT	(HF) 7,875lb
MAX SPEED	(F) 408mph at 16,000ft. 424mph at 29,500ft. (HF) 416mph at 44,000ft
CLIMB RATE (max)	4,060 ft/min
RANGE	660 miles
CEILING (service)	(HF) 45,100ft
CEILING (absolute)	45,700ft
ARMAMENT	'C' Type wing. Eight .303in machine guns and two or four 20mm Hispano cannon

Right: The prototype Spitfire Mk VII AB450, showing off its extended wingtips and twin cooling intakes under the wing. Other than the High Altitude Flight at Northolt, AB450 spent its days being developed by Supermarine and trialled by the A&AEE until the Summer of 1944. (Via Martyn Chorlton)

Below: The second of 164 production Mk VIIs, BS142 during trials at Boscombe Down in 1942. (Via Martyn Chorlton)

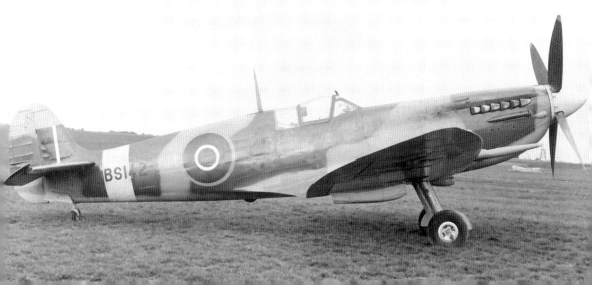

Spitfire F/LF/ HF Mk VIII & T Mk VIII

Development

Developed alongside the Mk VII, the MK VIII was virtually the same, with the addition of a pressurised cabin. Alongside its stable mate, the Mk VIII was also intended to become the main production model of the Spitfire, but the 'interim' Mk IX would steal the show, although this would not stop the Mk VIII from become the third most produced mark.

Design

The Mk VIII made full use of the Merlin 60 and 70 series to create three sub-variants that could operate at either high-altitude, low-level or standard general operations. The high-altitude HF Mk VIII retained the extended wingtips, the low-level LF had its wings clipped and the F had a traditional Spitfire wing fitted. One novel and undervalued feature of the new mark was a Voles Microvee air filter, which was a standard fit, to prevent dust and dirt entering the engine during desert and jungle operations. The filter was later used on all production Mk IXs.

The cockpit was revised on the later production models with a bubble canopy and a cut down rear fuselage significantly changing the look of the fighter. The redesign improved visibility, especially to rear.

T Mk VIII (T.8)

MT818 was the only example of Mk VII that was converted into a two-seat trainer to become a T Mk VIII, later T.8. Converted in 1946, the trainer was initially registered with Class B number N32 and then registered as G-AIDN. To accommodate a second, rear cockpit, the front was moved forward and the rear one was raised. It was demonstrated in many overseas countries but no orders were forthcoming. The aircraft survives today as the only example of a Spitfire prototype in existence.

Operational service

Despite the first Mk VIII flying for the first time in November 1942, the first did not enter service until June 1943 with 145 Squadron at Luqa, Malta, before fighting its way through Italy. The majority of Mk VIIIs were destined to serve in the Mediterranean or the Far East, the latter beginning with 155 Squadron, which received its new fighters in January 1944. The type arrived in the Far East just as the Japanese launched the Arakan offensive, supporting the Mk Vs already in theatre, which were a match for the enemy's best fighter, the Ki44 'Tojo'. However, the Mk VIII was faster and, between the two marks of Spitfire, the enemy was defeated in the air allowing the Allies to finally begin turning the tide against the Japanese.

The Mk VIII served with the following RAF units, 17, 20, 28, 32, 43, 54, 67, 73, 81, 87, 92, 94, 131, 132, 136, 145, 152, 153, 154, 155, 185, 208, 213, 238, 241, 253, 256, 273, 326, 327, 328, 417, 451, 452, 457, 548, 549, 601, 607 and 615 Squadrons. The mark was also flown by the RAAF by 79, 80, 417, 452 and 457 Squadrons. The 308th Fighter Squadron, 31st Fighter Group also operated the Mk VIII.

Production

In total, 1,600 F, LF and HF Mk VIIIs were built in six production batches during 1942 and 1944, all by Supermarine Aviation (Vickers). Serial ranges JF274-JG695, LV643-LV756, MB959-MD403, MT502-MV514, NH614-NH629 and PA952-PA958. One, ex-Mk VIII MT818, converted to T Mk VIII N-32/G-AIDN in 1946.

Technical data – Spitfire F/LF/HF Mk VIII and T Mk VIII	
ENGINE	(F) 1,565hp Rolls Royce Merlin 61 or 1,710hp Merlin 63 (LF) 1,580hp Merlin 66 (HF) 1,475hp Merlin 70 (T) 1,315hp Merlin 66
WINGSPAN	(F) 32ft 3in (LF) 36ft 10in (HF) 40ft 2in
LENGTH	30ft 4½in
WING AREA	(F & T) 242 sq ft (LF) 231 sq ft (HF) 248.5 sq ft
TARE WEIGHT	(F) 5,806lb (LF/HF) 5,805lb
TAKE-OFF WEIGHT	(F) 7,779lb. (LF/HF) 7,807lb
MAX WEIGHT	7,400lb
MAX SPEED	(F) 408mph, (LF) 362mph at sea level, (HF) 416mph. (T) 393 at 20,000ft
CLIMB	(LF) 25,000ft in 5.8 mins
CLIMB RATE (max)	5,100 ft/min. (T) 3,890ft/min at 18,000ft
RANGE	(F) 660 miles (T) 240 miles at 20,000ft
CEILING (service)	(F) 43,000ft, (LF) 41,500ft, (HF) 44,000ft. (T) 40,600ft
ARMAMENT	B wing. Some with Hispano Mk V cannon, 2 x 250lb or 1 500lb bomb

The prototype Mk VIII, JF299, was the first Spitfire to introduce the new tear-drop, or bubble, canopy and chopped down rear fuselage. (Via Martyn Chorlton)

Spitfire F/LF/HF Mk IX & T Mk IX

Development

The Spitfire Mk IX was yet another 'interim' that went on to be produced in huge numbers by Supermarine and Vickers-Armstrongs. The demand from the Air Ministry to raise the performance of the fighter to match the Fw 190 and Bf 109 saw the Spitfire receive the two-stage Merlin 60/70 series for the first time. The Mk VIII would not be produced in time, but conversions of the Mk II and Mk V with the new engine could.

Design

The Mk VC was chosen as the mark that would receive the Merlin 60/70 series with the least modifications and the facilities at Castle Bromwich were switched for production of the Mk IX. The first of three engines in series used was the 1,660hp Merlin 61, which was fitted into the F Mk IX. This variant was produced until 1943 and was followed by the Merlin 66 engine for the LF Mk IX, which was a better performer at lower altitude. The Merlin 70 was fitted into the HF Mk IX with better performance being achieved at a higher altitude.

The latest Spitfire was fitted with an intercooler radiator, which balanced the underwing ducting for the first time. The supercharger on the Merlin 60/70 series had a gear change that was introduced automatically by a barometric pressure 'aneroid', which helped to give the Mk IX a top speed 40mph faster than the Mk V and a climb rate of 4,000ft per minute. Comparison trials with a captured Fw 190 in July 1942 revealed that the Spitfire had closed the gap again and their capabilities were very similar.

The Mk IX also introduced the gyro gunsight for the first time and the 0.5in Browning machine gun, which was denoted by the suffix 'e' when fitted.

Operational service

The Mk IX entered RAF service with 64 Squadron at Hornchurch in July 1942 and, after suffering heavy losses, the type spearheaded the latest round of Circus, Ramrod and Rodeo operations. The first of many Fw 190s was shot down only a few days after the type entered service and, in September, a Mk IX carried out the highest interception of war at 43,000ft over Southampton. The mark also gained the distinction of becoming the first allied fighter to shoot down an Me262 when a 401 Squadron Mk IX claimed the kill on 5 October 1944.

By May 1945, there were still nine squadrons equipped with the Mk IX on home defence duties, five serving the 2nd TAF and 15 (including five with the SAAF) with both the Desert and Balkan Air Forces.

The Mk IX served with the following RAF squadrons, 1, 6, 16, 19, 32, 33, 43, 56, 64, 65, 66, 72, 73, 74, 80, 81, 87, 91, 92, 93, 94, 111, 118, 122, 123, 124, 126, 127, 129, 130, 131, 132, 133, 145, 152, 153, 154, 164, 165, 167, 183, 185, 208, 213, 222, 225, 229, 232, 234, 237, 238, 241, 242, 243, 249, 253, 256, 274, 287, 288, 302, 303, 306, 308, 310, 312, 313, 315, 316, 317, 318, 322, 326, 327, 328, 329, 331, 332, 336, 340, 341, 345, 349, 401, 402, 403, 411, 412, 414, 416, 417, 421, 441, 442, 443, 451, 453, 485, 501, 504, 521, 541, 595, 601, 602, 611, 680, 683 and 1435. The type also served with the FAA's 778 and 798 Squadrons.

Production

In total, 5,663 Spitfire Mk IXs were built by Supermarine and a further 557 by Vickers Armstrongs in 13 production batches from late 1940 through to late 1944.

Twenty T Mk IXs were built including the prototype G-ALJM. Six were delivered to the Irish Air Corps (IAC) in 1951, one to Egypt. Orders from Argentina and Iraq were cancelled.

Technical data – Spitfire F IXe	
ENGINE	(F) One 1,660hp Rolls-Royce 61. (HF) Merlin 70 (T) Merlin 266
WINGSPAN	36ft 10in
LENGTH	31ft ½in
HEIGHT (prop vertical, tail down)	11ft 8in
WING AREA	242 sq ft
TARE WEIGHT	5,800lb
LOADED WEIGHT	7,500lb
MAX SPEED	408mph at 25,000ft
CLIMB	20,000ft in 5.7 min
RATE OF CLIMB (initial)	3,950 ft/min
RANGE	434 miles at cruising speed of 324mph
CEILING (service)	43,000ft
ARMAMENT	Two 0.5in machine-guns, two 20mm Hispano cannon

Above left: Originally built as Mk VC, AB197, was the second prototype to be converted to a Mk IX with a Merlin 60 engine. Despite being the second, it was the first to fly on 26 February 1942. The fighter was used for a host of Mk IX related trials until it was SOC on 25 April 1944. (Via Martyn Chorlton)

Above right: A fine study of Spitfire Mk IXe MK126 of 126 Squadron with a 30-gallon slipper tank fitted. The fighter went on to serve with 56, 165 and 130 Squadrons before becoming an instructional airframe in November 1946. (*Aeroplane*)

Spitfire PR Mk X & XI

Development

Policy changes and changing priorities with regard to Spitfire fighter production resulted in the PR Mk X entering RAF service almost a year after the PR Mk XI. The cancellation of the PR.VIII also indirectly affected the proposed production of a pressurised high-altitude version of the Spitfire Mk VII delaying, the now renamed, PR Mk X. Based on the Mk VII airframe with a set of PR Mk XI wings and the same Universal Camera Installation, introduced with the PR Mk IV. It was fitted with a Lobelle (designed by Marcelle Lobelle) type sliding canopy but retained the fighter's bullet-proof windscreen and the guns were replaced with a pair of 66-gallon fuel tanks. Being pressurised, the PR Mk X had the ability to remain at heights above 40,000ft for longer periods of time without incapacitating the pilot. Power was provided by the two-stage supercharged Merlin 61.

The same delays that affected the PR Mk X also affected the PR Mk XI but for the latter it was a blessing in disguise. The new PR Mk XI was designed around the excellent Mk IX, rather than the VII and VIII, and was powered by the Merlin 60 series engine. However, it very nearly never happened at all and the series of PR Spitfires almost came to an end because of production problems. The Air Ministry quickly turned its attention to the Mosquito and proposed, prematurely, that all PR squadrons should be equipped with the type. In fact, a second report stated that 90% of all PR tasks could be carried out by the Mosquito, which would have brought all new Spitfire PR production to an end, as those remaining in service could have covered the remaining 10%. However, several senior members of the RAF were on the side of the Spitfire. The Air Ministry's mind was changed and it was decided that the PR Mk XI would, for the first time in Spitfire's history, be increased at the expense of the fighters.

The PR Mk XI utilised all the best features of the PR Mk VII, VIII and IX, the latter providing the fuselage. As in previous marks, it was fitted with the Universal Camera Installation, which gave the PR Mk XI the ability to operate at any altitude between 200 and 40,000ft!

Externally, the PR Mk XI differed little from previous marks with its deep nose, although the wrap-around windscreen was not armoured. 'Teardrop'-shaped fairings on the upper surface of each wing concealed a pair of booster fuel pumps and the tail wheel neatly retracted away once airborne. A four-blade Rotol propeller was turned by a Merlin 61 engine of which the first 260 produced were also fitted with the series 63 and 63A. The remaining 211 that were built were powered by the Merlin 70, which was designed to give more power at higher altitudes.

Operational service

The PR Mk XI entered service in February 1943 and remained the RAF's main recce Spitfire until December 1944 when it was superceded by the PR Mk XIX. However, several continued to serve until late 1946. Despite its earlier designation, the PR Mk X did not enter service until May 1944, serving with both 541 and 542 Squadrons before being withdrawn in late 1945. Both the PR Mk X and IX played an important role in the development of the forthcoming PR.XIX.

Production

Sixteen PR Mk Xs were built in the serial ranges MD191-MD199, MD213 and SR395 to SR400, the last (SR398) being delivered to 542 Squadron at Benson on 14 June 1944.

In total, 471 PR MK XIs and XITs (Tropical from October 1943) were built between late 1942 and early 1945.

Technical data – Spitfire PR Mk X and PR Mk XI	
ENGINE	(X) One 1,710hp Rolls-Royce Merlin 64 (XI) One 1,565hp Merlin 64, or 1,650hp Merlin 63, or 1,710hp Merlin 63A, or 1,475hp Merlin 70
WING AREA	242 sq ft
TARE WEIGHT	(X) 5,812lb (IX) 5,575lb (XIT) 5,602lb
TAKE-OFF WEIGHT (max)	(X) 8,159lb (XIT) 7,930lb (XI) 7,731lb
MAX SPEED	(X) 417mph at 24,200ft, 41mph at 28,000ft 387mph at 38,000ft (XI) (fully supercharged) 417mph at 31,000ft
CLIMB	(XI) 20,000ft in 5 min
RATE OF CLIMB (initial)	(XI) 4,250ft per/min
RANGE	(XI) 2,301 miles (ferry)
CEILING (service)	(XI) 44,000ft
ENDURANCE	(XI) 5.4hrs
CAMERA	(X) 2 x F.52 36in vertical mounted between frames 13 and 15. 10° 40in between each camera and each 5° 20in from the vertical, or 2 x F.8 20in or F.52 verticals, or 'W' installation 2 x F.24 14in and 1 x F.24 14 or 18in oblique. Heating hot air from radiator. (XI) Universal mounting, 2 x F.52 36in verticals, or 2 x F.8 20in and 1 x F.52 20in, or 2 x F.24 8in and 1 x F.24 8 or 14in. Heating hot air. Later aircraft had 1 x F.24 5in camera (one in each wing) between ribs 9 and 12 of the main spar. Each camera was covered by a blister fairing with a glass window protected by a metal mud flap.

Above left: First flown on 20 March 1943, three days later, PR Mk XI, EN427, arrived at Benson. By the following month the Spitfire was on the strength of 1 OADU at Portreath only to be mysteriously lost on an operation to Genoa on 29 August 1943. (Via Martyn Chorlton)

Above right: Rare colour photo of PR Mk XI, EN654, which was used for camera installation trials before delivery to 16 Squadron in October 1943. The aircraft was converted into a specially modified mail carrier, operating from Northolt in late 1945 before it was sold to the Ministry of Supply in August 1947. (Via Martyn Chorlton)

Spitfire LF Mk XII

Development

The Griffon engine had already been installed in DP845, an ex-Mk V that was developed as a Mk IV but redesignated as the Mk XX to avoid confusion with the PR Mk IV. The same aircraft, now with its wings clipped, became the prototype Mk XII in April 1942.

Design

The Griffon engine fitted into the Mk XII was bigger and longer than the Merlin 61 and was only fitted with a single-stage supercharger without an intercooler. Combined with a large spinner, a four-blade propeller and a bigger rudder to compensate for the increased side area, the Spitfire was now 31ft 10in long.

Speed was increased at lower levels to 372mph at 5,700ft and manoeuvrability was improved by clipping the wings as per the Mk III. The aircraft's longer nose and bigger engine reduced the pilot's forward visibility. To improve this, the top cowling was moulded over the cylinder banks to form a shallow v shape, giving the pilot a view between the curves of the upper fuselage. The big Griffon also forced the repositioning of the oil tank from under the crankcase to a location behind the fireproof bulkhead in front of the upper main fuel tank. The retractable tailwheel of the Mk III, twin wing fuel tanks, larger horn balances, torque-link undercarriage, leg fairings and strong four-spoke wheels were also fitted to the second production batch of aircraft.

Operational service

The Mk XII first entered service with 41 Squadron at High Ercall in February 1943, followed by 91 Squadron at Honiley in April. The Griffon-powered machine was a superb performer at low-level but Luftwaffe pilots were always wary of being drawn into combat by a Spitfire flying below 20,000ft. When they did engage, the Mk XII was very adept at dealing with Fw 190s and Bf 109Gs, especially during the enemy's hit and run raids along the south coast during late 1943 and early 1944.

The Mk XII's turn of speed also made it useful for dealing with the V-1, and 41 Squadron became quite adept at this task until they retired the type in September 1944 in favour of the excellent Mk XIV.

The Mk XII also served with 595 Squadron from December 1944 to July 1945 in the less glamorous role of anti-aircraft duties. At least one, EN226, served briefly with 778 Squadron in February/March 1943, most likely being trialled for potential use with the FAA, which never came to fruition. Several also continued useful service with the FLS at Milfield into 1945.

Production

One hundred Mk XIIs were built in two production batches by Supermarine under contract B19713/39. The serial ranges were EN221-EN238 (45) and MB794-MB805, MB829-MB863 and MB875-MB882 (55). The second batch was built between July 1943 and March 1944.

Technical data – Spitfire Mk XII	
ENGINE	One 1,735hp Rolls-Royce Griffon II, III or IV
SPAN	32ft 7in
LENGTH	31ft 10in
LOADED	7,400lb
MAX SPEED	372mph at 5,700ft 397mph at 18,000ft
CLIMB	20,000ft in 6.7 mins
RANGE	329 miles on 85 gallons. 493 miles on 113 gallons
CEILING	40,000ft
ARMAMENT	Two 20mm or four .303in machine guns and provision for 500lb of bombs

The graceful lines of the earlier Spitfires begin to fade with the introduction of the Griffon-powered Mk XII. This aircraft, MB878 was powered by a Griffon IV and is pictured during trials with a single 500lb bomb on a universal Mk II fuselage rack with the A&AEE in September 1943. (Via Martyn Chorlton)

MB858 and MB882, Mk XIIs of 41 Squadron, caught on patrol over the south coast during late 1943. MB858 ended its days at 33 MU, Lyneham, while MB882 was transferred to the Fighter Leaders School at Milfield in September 1944. (Via Martyn Chorlton)

Seafire F/LF & FR.III

Development

From the start, the Admiralty wanted a folding wing version of the Seafire and this finally came in 1943 with the F. III. This mark was the first fully adapted version for carrier operations and 1,263 were built, more than any other mark. The Seafire Mk III would serve the FAA in all theatres of war for the remainder of the conflict.

Design

Developed from the Seafire Mk IIC, the key and obvious difference over its predecessors was the folding wings. Supermarine's solution was a system of two straight chord wise folds with a break positioned outboard of the wheel-wells. At this point, the wing hinged vertically and at a slight angle towards the fuselage. The wingtips also folded downwards giving the F.III a width of just 13ft 4in and a height of 13ft 6in, making it ideal for stowage in the Royal Navy's below deck hangars.

Power was provided by the Merlin 55, which was fitted with an automatic boost control that gave the best performance possible at all altitudes. Following production problems, the Merlin 55M was also fitted. This engine produced more horse power at lower levels and all Seafires fitted with the 55M were designated as the LF.III.

Operational service

The Seafire III was first taken on charge by 894 Squadron on 27 November 1943, followed, not long after, by 801, 887, 889 and 880 Squadrons. The first major operation the mark was involved in was *Tungsten*. This was an air attack on the *Tirpitz* involving two waves of Barracudas with fighter protection contributed by 801 and 880 squadrons, both operating Seafire L.IIIs from HMS *Furious*. Planned for the 4 April 1944, the operation was launched a day early to catch the *Tirpitz* preparing for sea trials. Several hits were scored on the poorly defended ship causing damage that took two months to repair. There was no opposition from enemy aircraft and several FAA fighters (possibly including Seafires) managed to strafe the deck of the giant battleship.

Three squadrons, 808, 885 and 886 carried a different role during Operation *Overlord*. Because of an abundance of Allied fighter units, the FAA's Seafire IIIs were tasked with providing air spotting for the allied warships throughout the invasion under the control of the 2nd TAF.

The Seafire III's finest hour came during the closing stages of World War Two against the Japanese in the Pacific. The LF.III was particular suited to this theatre, especially against the kamikaze threat that often saw the enemy approaching at 'zero' feet.

The following units operated the Seafire III with the FAA from November 1943 to March 1946; 700, 706, 708, 709, 715, 718, 721, 728, 733, 736, 736B, 740, 744, 748, 757, 759, 760, 761, 766, 767, 768, 771, 772, 778, 781, 782, 787, 787Y, 790, 794, 798, 799, 801, 802, 803, 805, 806, 807, 808, 809, 879, 880, 883, 885, 886, 887, 889, 894, 899 and 1832 Squadrons.

An order for a dozen Seafire IIIs was signed on 31 August 1946 by the IAC, numbered 146 to 157. All naval equipment was removed and the aircraft were actually delivered as Mk VCs. The majority remained in IAC service until 1955.

Forty-eight Seafire IIIs were also transferred to the French Navy in 1946 for use on their aircraft Colossus.

Production

1,263 Seafire Mk IIIs were built in eight production batches by Westland and Cunliffe Owen. Westland built 913 in five production orders and Cunliffe Owen built the remaining 350 in two. The aircraft were serialled with the following prefixes, LR, NF, NM, NN, PP, PR, PX, RX and SP. They were all built between January 1943 and March 1945.

Technical data – Seafire F.III	
ENGINE	(F) One 1,585hp Rolls-Royce Merlin 55M
WINGSPAN	36ft 10in (folded, width): 13ft 4in
LENGTH	30ft 2½in
HEIGHT (prop vertical, tail down)	11ft 5½in (wings folded): 13ft 6in
WING AREA	242 sq ft
TARE WEIGHT	5,317lb
LOADED WEIGHT	7,232lb
MAX SPEED	359mph at 36,000ft
CLIMB	20,000ft in 8.1 min
RATE OF CLIMB (initial)	3,250 ft/min
RANGE	465 miles at cruising speed of 272mph
CEILING (service)	36,000ft
ARMAMENT	Four .303in machine-guns, two 20mm Hispano cannon. Two 250lb or a single 500lb bomb
CAMERAS	(FR) Two F.24 cameras

Above left: Seafire III NF545, powered by a Merlin 55M, pictured only days before the fighter was delivered to 899 Squadron on 17 March 1944. By May the Seafire was on board HMS *Ravager* en route to Gibraltar but, by August, was back in Britain with the A&AEE at Boscombe Down. (Via Martyn Chorlton)

Above right: Seafire III, NF547 of 885 Squadron demonstrating the type's useful ability to fold its wings at Henstridge in May 1944. This fighter had a busy and successful career, being credited with one Bf109 shot down near Caen (Sub Lt R C S Chamen SANF) in June 1944 and two others damaged. The aircraft was later transferred to 899 and 709 Squadrons before being SOC in August 1945. (Via Martyn Chorlton)

Spitfire F/FR Mk XIV

Development

The next Griffon-powered Spitfire to enter production was the Mk XIV, which was based on the Mk VIII airframe. The idea was that the Mk XIV would bridge the production gap before the redesigned Mk XVIII was made available. Once again though, as with nearly all 'interim' Spitfires, the protracted development of their replacement meant that the temporary designs became the most useful.

Design

The Mk XIV was designed for high-altitude combat and was powered by a 2,035hp Griffon 65 engine driving a Rotol five-blade propeller. The Griffon 65 was fitted with a two-stage two-speed supercharger and an intercooler making it a good performer at all altitudes. The combination of the Griffon and the five-blade propeller, which was designed for the best possible thrust above 30,000ft, made the Mk XIV a real threat to the enemy at higher altitude.

The bigger engine gave the Mk XIV a longer nose, which was not a huge issue, as the Mk VIII fuselage was already modified to cope with the length of the Merlin 61.

The long nose was compensated by a larger area fin and rudder and control surfaces were modified, including repositioning the ailerons further inboard to give better lateral control.

Six prototypes, ex-Mk VIIIs JF316 to JF321 were converted to Mk XIV standard. Early production aircraft were built with the standard Spitfire rear fuselage, while later models were chopped down with a bubble canopy.

The Mk XIVe introduced the 'universal armament' wing while the FR Mk XIVe, the fighter-reconnaissance version, had its wings clipped to 32ft 8in.

Operational service

The Mk XIV first entered service with 610 Squadron at Exeter in January 1944, followed by moves to Culmhead and Fairwood Common. The unit settled at West Malling. It was from the latter that the mark began its campaign against the V-1 flying-bomb threat. Only beaten by the Tempest Mk V for performance, the Spitfire Mk XIV Wing (41, 91, 130, 350 and 610 Squadrons) went on to shoot down 300 V-1s of the 429 claimed by all home-defence Spitfires of all marks. 91 Squadron, which operated the type from March 1944, managed to claim 184 alone!

The Mk XIV also equipped several squadrons of the 2nd TAF from September 1944 including 2,268, 401 and 402, all flying the FR XIVe. The latter proved particularly useful, flying armed reconnaissance operations hunting for enemy targets behind the German lines.

From the end of 1946, Mk XIVs were serving with the Royal Auxiliary Air Force with 600, 602, 610, 611 and 612 Squadrons. The type also served in the Far East with 17 and 132 Squadrons of 902 (Madras) Wing from May 1945.

The Mk XIV served with 36 squadrons; they were 2, 11, 16, 17, 20, 26, 28, 41, 91, 130, 132, 136, 152, 155, 268, 273, 322, 350, 401, 402, 403, 411, 412, 414, 416, 430, 443, 451, 600, 602, 607, 610, 611, 612, 613 and 615.

The Mk XIV also saw service with the Royal Belgian, Indian and Thai Air Force.

Production

Total production of the Mk XIV totalled 963, including the six prototypes JF316-JF321. The production aircraft were built with the following serial prefixes, MT, MV, NH, NM, RB, RM, RN, SM, TP, TX and TZ.

Technical data – Spitfire Mk XIV	
ENGINE	One 2,035hp Rolls-Royce Griffon 65
WINGSPAN	36ft 10in (FR) 32ft 8in
WINGSPAN	36ft 10in (FR) 32ft 8in
LENGTH	32ft 8in
HEIGHT (prop vertical, tail down)	11ft 8¼in
WING AREA	242 sq ft
TARE WEIGHT	6,576lb
LOADED WEIGHT	8,475lb
MAX SPEED	439mph at 24,500ft
CLIMB	20,000ft in 7 min
RATE OF CLIMB (initial)	4,580 ft/min
RANGE	465 miles at cruising speed of 271mph
CEILING (service)	43,000ft
ARMAMENT	(XIVe) B wing with two .5in machine-guns, two 20mm Hispano cannon. Plus Mk IX RP, 250lb, 500lb or 120lb (smoke) bombs

Above left: The third prototype Spitfire Mk XIV, JF318, was a troubled machine that was plagued with continual problems from its Griffon 61 engine. Although it was replaced, the second engine failed after just 47 hours, causing a force landing. When a third engine failed on 23 September 1943, the aircraft had to be abandoned to crash near Amesbury Cemetery. (Via Martyn Chorlton)

Above right: Spitfire Mk XIV RM701 which served with 41 Squadron during the unit's V-1 campaign and then post-war with the Belgian Air Force as 'SG-6'.

Spitfire PR Mk XIII

Development

Converted from the Mk IIA, V and PR Mk VIIs, the PR Mk XIII was developed as a low-level reconnaissance fighter. Despite only being produced in small numbers, the mark would make a name for itself over the beaches of Normandy in 1944.

Design

Twenty-eight aircraft were converted by Heston Aircraft in 1943 to PR Mk XIII standard with the same camera fit as the earlier PR Type G, with two vertical and one oblique F.24 cameras. A 1,645hp Rolls-Royce Merlin 32 (Merlin 45 in last two aircraft) was fitted, which was specifically rated for low-altitude operations. An armament of four .303in machine guns, in the two outer positions, was fitted for defensive purposes and an additional 29 gallon fuel tank was installed behind the cockpit.

Operational service

The prototype PR Mk XIII was ex-Mk IA L1004 that first flew in February 1943. Without delay, the first PR Mk XIII to enter service arrived with 542 Squadron at Benson in April. The mark also appeared with 4, 400, 540 and 541 Squadrons. As the PR Mk XIII was a rare machine, only a few ever served with each unit and as such, are not credited as being on strength within their respective histories.

The PR MK XIIIs main operational area was Northern Europe because of its limited, as far as photo-reconnaissance aircraft were concerned, range of 700 miles. This did not stop the mark from playing a valuable contribution during Operation *Overlord* in June 1944, where it photographed the beaches at very low level before the invasion took place.

A handful of PR Mk XIIIs also served with the FAA including 718 Squadron (June 1944 to October 1945), 761 Squadron (March to June 1944), 808 Squadron (March 1944) and 886 Squadron (March 1944).

Production

A single prototype, ex-Mk IA L1004 ordered as Type 367/1 and issued 30 September 1942. 28 aircraft were converted to PR MK XIII standard by Heston Aircraft with the following serials, P7505, P8784, R7308, R7335, W3112, W3135, W3831, X4021, X4615, X4660, X4766, AA739, AD354, AD389, AD501, AD556, AR212, AR319, AR620-AR621, BL446, BL526, BL738, BM350, BM447, BM591, EN902 and EP229. All, except the prototype were converted from MK IIA, Mk V and PR Mk VII.

Technical data – Spitfire PR Mk XIII	
ENGINE	One 1,645hp Rolls-Royce Merlin 32
WINGSPAN	32ft 2in
LENGTH	29ft 11in
WING AREA	231 sq ft
TAKE-OFF WEIGHT	6,353lb
MAX SPEED	342mph at 4,000ft, 335mph at 20,000ft, 327mph at 24,000ft
CLIMB	34,000ft in 23.5 mins, 20,000ft in 6.65 mins
RANGE	700 miles
CEILING (service)	35,000ft
CAMERA	'G' installation as per PR Mk VII
ARMAMENT	'A' wing. Four .303in machine guns. Later production examples carried 350rpg and were fitted with four outer guns only
CAMERAS	Two vertical F.24 cameras and one oblique F.24 camera

The prototype PR Mk XIII ex-Mk IA L1004 pictured at Boscombe Down in March 1943. It first flew in its latest guise on 16 February 1943 before carrying out weight, centre of gravity, climb, speed and diving trials with the A&AEE. The aircraft was later converted into the Seafire III prototype. (Via Martyn Chorlton)

Spitfire Mk XVI

Development

The last of a very long line of Merlin-powered Spitfires saw the arrival of the Mk XVI. The fighter's roots were firmly embedded in the Mk IX, which was constantly being modified to a point when it was fitted with a Packard Merlin engine, justifying the Spitfire being redesignated with a different mark.

Design

Built by the Packard car company, the license built version of the Merlin had been coming off the production lines in American since late 1940. The version destined for the Mk XVI was the 1,705hp Merlin 266, which was similar to the British-built Merlin 66. The only obvious external modification for the American-built unit was a bulged upper cowling to cover the engine's taller intercooler.

The Mk XVI was built with a standard and clipped wing (the majority) as per the Mk IX and late production aircraft, from February 1945, featured a chopped down rear fuselage and a sliding bubble canopy. Additional rear fuselage tanks had a combined capacity of 75 gallons; the bubble canopy versions, however, had smaller tanks with a capacity of 66 gallons.

Operational service

A single prototype, MJ556 was fitted with the first Packard Merlin 266 in December 1943 and the first flew not long after.

The Mk XIV first entered RAF service in November 1944 with 602 Squadron at Matlask. Some of 602 Squadron's early operations from Coltishall saw the mark flying against V2 rocket sites. Another 51 RAF squadrons would go on to be equipped with the Mk XIV which, by May 1945, was serving with four squadrons of Fighter Command and eleven of 2nd TAF. Seven Royal Auxiliary Air Force squadrons operated the type which served with several Anti-Aircraft Co-operation units until 1951.

RAF Mk XVI squadrons were, 5, 16, 17, 19, 20, 31, 34, 63, 65, 66, 74, 126, 164, 229, 287, 288, 302, 303, 308, 317, 322, 329, 340, 341, 345, 349, 350, 401, 402, 403, 411, 412, 416, 421, 443, 451, 501, 567, 577, 587, 595, 601, 602, 603, 604, 609, 612, 614, 631, 667, 691 and 695.

Production

The Mk XVI entered production in September 1944 and continued through to August 1945. In total, 1,053 Mk XVIs were built, all at Castle Bromwich, in the serial prefix ranges: PV, RK, RR, RW, SL and SM.

Technical data – Spitfire Mk XVI, and XVIe	
ENGINE	One 1,720hp Packard Merlin 266
WINGSPAN	32ft 8in
LENGTH	31ft 4in
WING AREA	242 sq ft
TARE WEIGHT	5,894lb
TAKE-OFF WEIGHT	8,288.5lb
MAX WEIGHT (overload)	9,500lb
MAX SPEED	405mph at 22,000ft
RATE OF CLIMB	3,970ft/min
RANGE	434 miles with 85 gallons. 721 miles with 175 gallons
ARMAMENT	(XVI) Two 20mm and four 0.303in machine guns. (XVIe) Two 20mm and two 0.5in machine guns. Provision for 1,000lb of bombs or RPs

Right: RW396, a LF Mk XVIe displaying the codes of the Central Gunnery School at Leconfield captured over the Yorkshire coast. Not long after this photo was taken, and not far either, the fighter suffered an engine failure and force landed at West Skipsea Ranges on 1 January 1949. (Via Martyn Chorlton)

Below: 421 (Red Indian) Squadron Mk XIVe *Dorothy II* at B154/Reinsehlen in May 1945. (Via Martyn Chorlton)

Spitfire PR Mk XIX

Development

Increasing experience and information gained from the operations flown by the PR Mk XI resulted in even more development. Despite the increased performance at altitude of the Merlin 70, PR Mk XI pilots were finding it increasingly difficult to maintain a height advantage over the defending Luftwaffe fighters. To increase the advantage, it was obvious that a new aircraft with a new engine was needed, the latter being provided by the Rolls-Royce Griffon.

Not only was more power needed above 40,000ft but, to deal with this altitude, it was essential that the cockpit be pressurised. In March 1944, as a temporary measure, Supermarine also provided the RAF with 16 PR Mk XIs which were modified with pressurised cockpits. These were to be followed by 22 Griffon 65 powered, non-pressurised PR Mk XIs as outlined in an earlier specification. This batch would be redesignated into the final mark of RAF Reconnaissance Spitfire, the PR Mk XIX.

Design

The PR Mk XIX probably utilised more components from previous marks than any other Spitfire produced, making it the ultimate hybrid. The aircraft's chassis was from a Mk VIII and XIV, the fuselage was also a Mk XIV with a PR Mk XI screen. The wings were the D Type 'Bowser' as per a PR Mk XI and the list goes on with regard to subsidiary components. Power for the initial batch of PR Mk XIXs was provided by the Griffon 65 driving a Rotol five blade wooden propeller.

Camera fits for both versions of the PR Mk XIX was, by now, the standard Universal Camera Installation. At this stage of the war, the two vertical cameras were either F.52s with a 20in lens or a pair of F.8s with either a 14 or 30in lens. The aircraft's performance had come a long way since the PR.I – the PR.XIX was capable of operating up to 42,600ft and had a top speed of 445mph at 26,000ft.

Operational service

RM626 was the first PR Mk XIX to enter RAF service with 106 Group on 16 May 1944. The first operational sortie was flown by Sqn Ldr Bell of 542 Sqn on 24 May over Le Havre in support of the forthcoming invasion. Of these early PR Mk XIXs, the vast majority served with 541 and 542 Squadrons out of Benson.

The PR Mk XIX was destined to serve the RAF long after the end of World War Two. In fact, it was PR Mk XIX, PS888, of 81 Squadron that flew the very last Spitfire operational sortie on 1 April 1954 while serving at Seletar during the Malayan campaign. The last serving RAF Spitfire was also a PR Mk XIX, PS853, which, along with two others, PM631 and PS915, served with the THUM (Temperature and Humidity) Flight based at Woodvale making its last flight on 10 June 1957. Once this unit disbanded, the three aircraft were flown to Biggin Hill on 11 July 1957 to join the fledgling Historic Aircraft Flight, now known as the BBMF. Today, PS915 and PM631, both serve with the BBMF, while PS853 is operated by Rolls-Royce Heritage Trust in flying condition.

Production

22 PR Mk XIXs were ordered on 27 March 1944 within the serial ranges PM496-PM519, PM536-PM637, PM651-PM661, PS831-PS836, PS849-PS893, PS908-PS935 and RM626-RM646. An order for a single pressurised PR Mk XIX, SW777 was placed in March 1944.

Technical data – Spitfire PR Mk XIX	
ENGINE	One 2,035hp Rolls-Royce Griffon 66
WINGSPAN	36ft 10in
LENGTH	32ft 8in
WING AREA	242 sq ft
TARE WEIGHT	6,550lb
TAKE-OFF WEIGHT	8,575lb
MAX WEIGHT	10,450lb
MAX SPEED	460mph
RATE OF CLIMB (initial)	4,400 ft/min
RANGE	1,010 miles at 325–360mph at 35,000ft
CEILING (service)	42,600ft
CAMERA	a) 2 x F.52 36in fanned vertical. b) 1 x F.52 vertical. c) 2 x F.52 20in fanned vertical. d) 2 x F.8 20in fanned vertical. e) 2 x F.24 14 in vertical or, f) 1 x F.24 14 or 18in port facing oblique

Above: PS925 pictured serving with the Photographic Reconnaissance Development Unit based at Benson between December 1943 and August 1947. The aircraft crashed on approach to Leuchars on 1 July 1949 while serving with 237 OCU. (Via Martyn Chorlton)

Right: PR Mk XIX PM631 in company with Hurricane IIC LF363. Both aircraft are still serving with the BBMF based at Coningsby in Lincolnshire. (Via Gerry O' Neill)

Spiteful

Development

Back in November 1942, Supermarine produced Specification 470 which was specifically written for a Spitfire with a laminar flow wing. The wing was given its own type No.371, a number which was later transferred to the Spiteful as a whole. The objectives of the specification were 'to raise as much as possible the critical speed at which drag increases due to compressibility and to obtain a rate of roll faster than any existing fighter and to reduce profile drag, thereby improving performance.

History

The wing section for the Spiteful was developed with the help of the National Physical Laboratory (NPL) at Bushy Park, Teddington, and was designed to maintain laminar flow as far back as possible, avoiding hindrance from the slipstream and/or projecting gun barrels. The wing was no thicker than 42% of the chord and a aileron reversal speed of 850mph was the target. The Spiteful's wing was reduced in area to 210 sq/ft and its straight leading and trailing edges made production simple and gave it a conventional two-spar design. The wing would also be 200lb lighter than the Spitfire F.21 and it was hoped performance could increase by 55mph.

Three prototypes were ordered under Specification F.1/43, which called for the laminar flow wing and a contra-rotating propeller. The Spiteful was designed to carry 149 gallons of fuel plus 60 gallons more with drop tanks. Fitted with a rear-view sliding hood, the fighter was to have provision for folding wings for potential FAA operation. The two-spar design made this easier than the earlier single-spar Spitfire wing. The two-spar wing also allowed for an inwards-retracting undercarriage, which raised the original narrow track of the Spitfire by 4ft.

Operational service

After extensive wind-tunnel trials, the laminar flow wing was fitted to Spitfire Mk XIV NN660 and was first flown by Jeffrey Quill on 30 June 1944. Inexplicably, the aircraft was lost on 13 September during a flight from High Post, killing the experienced Supermarine test pilot Frank Furlong. The second prototype, NN664, which was built as the first full production version of the Spiteful to specification F.1/43, first flew on 8 January 1945 in the hands of Jeffrey Quill. Before NN660 crashed, a large amount of information had been gained from the aircraft including 'snatching' ailerons, the drop of a wing just before the stall, and an alarming 'flick' during the stall when under high g-forces. It was obvious that the new laminar flow wing on its own was not going to be the answer to pushing on into transonic flight.

After a plethora of modifications and flight trials using NN664, it was clear that the performance increase over the Spitfire that was hoped for could not be achieved. However, the wing performed as it should and would be used in jet aircraft in the near future.

The first production aircraft, RB515, flew in April 1945 and, along with several early Spitefuls, they were all used for trials to improve the aerodynamics of the laminar flow wing. Fitted with a short air intake, a Griffon 69 engine and a Rotol five-blade propeller, the aircraft was designated as the F.14. The Griffon 89 or 90-powered aircraft with the originally specified six-blade contra-rotating propeller was designated as the F.15. The one and only F.16, RB518, was powered by a three-speed Griffon 101 fitted with a five-blade Rotol. RB518 was by far the highest performer, reaching 494mph after the Griffon's boost was pushed to 25lb.

Production

Large contracts were issued between February and July 1943 but the result was just 19 aircraft including two prototypes. NN660 and NN664, the two prototypes, were ordered on 6 February 1943 from converted Spitfire VIIIs.

Technical data – Spiteful F.1	
ENGINE	One 2,375hp Rolls-Royce Griffon 69
WINGSPAN	35ft
LENGTH	32ft 11in
HEIGHT	13ft 5in
WING AREA	210 sq ft
TARE WEIGHT	7,350lb
LOADED WEIGHT	9,950lb
MAX SPEED	483mph at 21,000ft
RATE OF CLIMB (initial)	4,890 ft/min
RANGE	564 miles at 240-255mph
CEILING (service)	42,000ft
ARMAMENT	Four 20mm Hispano cannon with 624 rounds and provision for two 1,000lb or four 300lb RPs, a pair under each wing

The hybrid prototype Spiteful NN660, which was effectively a Mk XIV, fitted with a Supermarine Type 371 laminar flow wing. The fighter was lost on 13 September 1944, taking the life of Supermarine test pilot Frank Furlong with it. Furlong, a former steeplechase jockey, won the 1935 Grand National. (Via Martyn Chorlton)

Spitfire F.21

Development

As early as 1942 the Spitfire was subjected to a major redesign which resulted in the F.21. This mark was destined to be the last of the breed to see wartime service. The arrival of the powerful Griffon 61 engine meant that the Spitfire would have be built considerably stronger, to harness the 2,000hp plus now available.

Design

A new wing was designed for the F.21 which was 47% stiffer than previous marks. This resulted in a theoretical aileron reversal speed of 850mph and a potential role rate of 120° per second at 300mph. The old Frise type ailerons were replaced by ones that were 5% bigger and were attached to the wing by a continuous, single hinge.

A five-blade 11ft diameter propeller (7in bigger than the Mk XIV) was attached to the Griffon engine. The bigger propeller would need more ground clearance and this was achieved by making the undercarriage legs 4.5in longer. This then created the problem of retracting the longer legs into the wheel wells, and this was solved by a complex system of hydraulic levers which shortened them by 8in as they were raised. Stronger, four-spoke wheels were fitted to deal with the extra weight of the fighter and the undercarriage was spaced by an extra 7¾in, to improve handling during taxying, take-off and landing.

Operational service

DP851, originally built as an Mk IV was the first aircraft converted into a F.21, with a Griffon 61 engine as far back as October 1942. The first 'true' F.21 prototype, PP139 first flew in July 1943 and during early flight trials with the A&AEE, the design differences over the Spitfire caused the establishment to refer to aircraft as the 'Victor'. The first production aircraft, LA187, powered by a Griffon 65 first flew in March 1944. During further flight testing by both the A&AEE and AFDU, the F.21 was found to be over sensitive to trim changes and handling was described as unsatisfactory for use as a fighter. One report by the AFDU dared to suggest that further development of the Spitfire should cease. By this stage the F.21 was already leaving the Castle Bromwich production line and was about to enter operational service. Following further intensive test flying the problems were ironed out by adjusting the gearing of the trim tabs and other minor control modifications.

The F.21 first entered service with 91 Squadron at Manston in January 1945 followed by 1 Squadron at Ludham in May. 91 Squadron managed to squeeze in 154 operational sorties before the war ended, including a novel action on 26 April when the unit claimed a German midget submarine sunk. Post-war the F.21 also served with 41, 122, 595, 600, 602 and 615 Squadrons and the CFE.

Production

In total, 3,000 F.21s were ordered, but only 120 were actually built, in the serial ranges DP851 (the prototype), LA187-LA236, LA249-LA284, LA299 to LA332 and PP139.

Technical data – Spitfire F.21	
ENGINE	One 2,050hp Rolls-Royce Griffon 61 and 65
WINGSPAN	36ft 11in
LENGTH	32ft 8in
HEIGHT (prop vertical, tail down)	11ft 9¾in
WING AREA	243.6 sq ft
TARE WEIGHT	6,923lb
LOADED WEIGHT	9,182lb
MAX SPEED	450mph at 19,000ft
CLIMB	20,000ft in 8 min
RATE OF CLIMB (initial)	4,900 ft/min
RANGE	580 miles at cruising speed of 230mph
CEILING (service)	43,000ft
ARMAMENT	Four 20mm Hispano Mk II cannon with 150 rpg

First flown on 30 December 1944, the F.21 is pictured wearing the code letters of the Central Fighter Establishment. Note the starboard undercarriage door refuses to retract! (Via Martyn Chorlton)

Spitfire F/FR Mk XVIII 'Super Spitfire'

Development

The Mk XVIII was the final stage in a long chain that began with the Mk VII, followed by the Mk VIII and Mk XIV. While not the last of the breed, the mark saw the final use of the classic elliptical wing, which had been the hall mark of the Spitfire since its arrival in 1936.

Design

With its strengthened wings, undercarriage and bubble canopy, the Mk XVIII, at first glance, was not dissimilar to a later production Mk XIV. Power was supplied by a Griffon 65 and 67 and fuel capacity was increased thanks to an extra 26½ gallons of fuel in the wings and 66 gallons in the rear fuselage.

The mark was produced in two versions; the 'F', standard fighter and the 'FR', a fighter-reconnaissance version. The latter could carry a pair of oblique and a single vertical F.24 or an F.52 in the vertical on its own. The 'FR' retained the 'E' type wing's armament of a pair of 20mm cannons and two 0.5in machine guns or four 20mm cannon. The fighter variant had the same armament options but was fitted with a clipped wing.

Operational service

The first Mk XVIIIs entered service with 208 Squadron at Ein Shemar, Palestine, in August 1946. They were tasked with flying operations against Jewish terrorist organisations but later on, in May 1948, the enemy was the Egyptian Air Force. Flying Spitfire Mk IXs, the Egyptians attacked the airfield at Ramat David on 20 May, believing it to be occupied by Israeli forces but, it was actually occupied by 208 Squadron and several other RAF units, on detachment from Nicosia. Two Mk XVIIIs of 32 Squadron were destroyed on the ground but five days later, during another attempted attack by the Egyptians, five of their number was shot down by 208 Squadron.

On 7 January 1949, whilst carrying out a reconnaissance close to the Egyptian/Israeli border, a 208 Squadron Mk XVIII was brought down by anti-aircraft fire. Three other Spitfires on the same sortie were then bounced by Spitfires of 101 Squadron, Israeli Air Force, and all shot down in the Sinai Desert. Three out of the four 208 Squadron pilots survived.

Mk XVIIIs also served with 60 Squadron during Operation *Firedog* in Malaya from January 1947. It was these aircraft that flew the last operational Spitfire 'fighter' sortie in May 1951 before being replaced by Vampires.

The MK XVIII also served with 28, 31, and 81 Squadrons and a handful saw service with Burmese and Indian Air Forces.

Production

In all, 300 Mk XVIIIs were built, made up of 100 F Mk XVIIIs and 200 FR Mk XVIIIs in the following serial ranges, NH847-NH856 and NH872, SM843-SM845, SM939-SM936 and SM968-SM997, TP195-TP235, TP257-TP298, TP313-TP350, TP363-TP408 AND TP423-TP456, TZ200-TZ205 and TZ210-TZ240.

Technical data – Spitfire MK XVIII	
ENGINE	One 2,035hp Rolls-Royce Griffon 65 or 2,340hp Griffon 67
WINGSPAN	36ft 10in
LENGTH	33ft 3¼in
WING AREA	242 sq ft
LOADED WEIGHT	9,320lb
MAX SPEED	442mph
RATE OF CLIMB (initial)	5,000 ft/min
CEILING	41,000ft
CAMERA	(FR) One x F.24 14in oblique and two x F.24 20in verticals, or one x F.52 vertical
ARMAMENT	Two 20mm and two 0.5in machine guns and up to 1,000lb of bombs. 'E' wing. Plus 3 x 500lb GP bombs or Mk VIII and Mk IX RPs. Plus 60lb (25lb head), 100 (60), 180 (60)lb rockets, also 300 (180)

Right: A rare shot of FR Mk XVIII, TP318, in service with 208 Squadron, which dates this photo between February 1950 and February 1952 when it was SOC. (Via Martyn Chorlton)

Below: Spitfire Mk XVIII, NH872, was put through extensive testing by the A&AEE from late 1944 through to late 1945, eventually contributing to the Spitfire F.21's development. Pictured here in June 1945, the fighter was sold as scrap on 20 January 1954. (Via Martyn Chorlton)

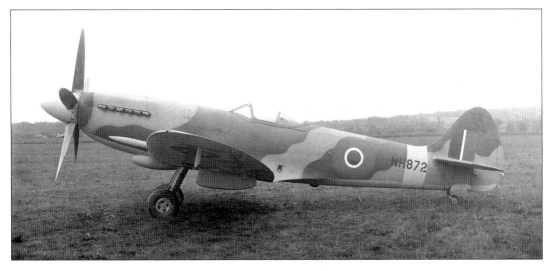

Spitfire F.22

Development

A development of the F.21, the F.22 differed in appearance by having a tear-drop canopy and a cut-down rear fuselage. After initial instability problems the mark went on to become the backbone of the re-formed Royal Auxiliary Air Force from 1947 to 1951.

Design

The introduction of the tear-drop canopy and modified rear fuselage introduced the problem of instability which had been experienced with the F.21. This problem was rectified by enlarging the tail surfaces in a similar fashion to the Seafire F.46 which was being developed at the same time. Control surfaces were increased by more than 25% as a result.

Power was provided by the Griffon 85 driving a six-blade contra-rotating propeller. The F.21's 12 volt electrical system was uprated to 24 volts as well.

Operational service

The Spitfire F.22 first entered RAF service with 73 Squadron at Ta Kali, Malta, in July 1947. This was to be the regular RAF unit operating the type, which had a short service life, being withdrawn in October 1948 following the arrival of the Vampire F.3, three months earlier.

The F.22 did make its presence felt with the Royal Auxiliary Air Force with which it equipped ten squadrons. The first to receive the type was 603 (City of Edinburgh) Squadron based at Turnhouse in May 1948. The rest, 500, 502, 504, 600, 602, 607, 608, 610, 611, 613, 614 and 615 Squadrons received their new Spitfires between May 1948 and January 1949. By 1951, all of the auxiliaries had been re-equipped with the Vampire F.1, F.3 or FB.5 or the Meteor F.4.

Several F.22s were relegated to second line training units and refresher schools, serving on until May 1955.

Refurbished examples were also sold to the Egyptian, Syrian and Southern Rhodesian Air Forces.

Production

278 F.22s were built, the majority at Castle Bromwich and a handful at South Marston in the following serial ranges, PK312-PK356, PK369-PK412, PK426-PK435, PK481-PK525, PK539-PK582, PK594-PK635, PK648-PK677, PK680, PK684 and PK715. PK678-PK689 and PK712-PK726 built as F.24s instead.

Technical data – Spitfire F.22	
ENGINE	One 2,050hp Rolls-Royce Griffon 85
WINGSPAN	36ft 11in
LENGTH	32ft 11in
WING AREA	244 sq ft
LOADED WEIGHT	9,900lb
MAX SPEED	454mph at 26,000ft
CLIMB	20,000ft in 8 min
RATE OF CLIMB	3,600 ft/min
RANGE	490 miles on 120 gallons, 640 miles on 150 gallons or 880 miles on 210 gallons
CEILING (service)	43,500ft
ARMAMENT	Four 20mm Hispano Mk 2 cannon 175rpg inner, 150 outer. Plus 3 x 500lb bombes, three sets of rockets 60, 100, 2 x 60, 180, 2 x 100

Above: The prototype Spitfire F.22 PK312, which first flew on 21 March 1945 and spent the next two years flying development trials, including being fitted with a Spiteful tail unit, before being SOC on 18 April 1947. (Via Martyn Chorlton)

Right: F.22 PK523 pictured following its refurbishment by Airwork General Trading at Gatwick on 4 June 1951. The fighter had served with 608 (North Riding) Squadron at Thornaby. (Via Martyn Chorlton)

Spitfire F.24

Development

The Spitfire F.24 marks the culmination of ten years' worth of development, which saw the fighter double in weight and become twice as powerful. The latter was mainly achieved through the introduction of the Griffon engine which, despite early development problems, blossomed into a unit that could now boast more than 2,000hp.

Design

The Spitfire F.24 was basically an F.22 that incorporated a few key features. Firstly, the F.24 had a greater fuel capacity, being fitted with a pair of 33-gallon fuel tanks in the rear fuselage. The F.24 was also fitted with a Spiteful tail, which had its trim tab gears modified to suit the handling of the fighter.

Armament capability was also improved through zero-length fittings under each wing for RPs and some of the later production aircraft were fitted with light, short-barrelled Hispano Mk V cannons. These modifications made the F.24 a more versatile combat aircraft than its predecessors, allowing it to be used in a variety of offensive roles. As a fighter, the new Hispano cannon packed the punch that was needed to bring down heavily armoured opponents. As a fighter-bomber, the F.24 was more than capable of carrying a single 500lb or a pair of 250lb bombs as well as eight RPs.

The F.24's blistering performance made it the equal of all other piston engined fighters of the day. The Griffon 61 engine gave the F.24 a top speed of 454mph and 30,000ft could be reached in just eight minutes.

Operational service

The F.24 first entered service with 80 Squadron at Wunstorf, West Germany, in January 1948, destined to become the RAF's only operational unit to fly the type. After service with BAFO, the squadron transferred to the Far East Air Force, setting sail aboard HMS *Ocean* on 14 July 1949 bound for Hong Kong. The F.24 was operated from Kai Tak and Sek Kong until December 1951, being replaced by the Hornet F.3.

Nine F.24s enjoyed extended service with the Royal Hong Kong Auxiliary Air Force from early 1952 through to 1955.

Production

There were 81 F.24s, and the following serials were converted from F.22s: PK678-PK679, PK681-PK683, PK685-PK689, PK712-PK714 and PK716-PK726. VN301-VN334 and VN477-VN496 (54 aircraft) were built as F.24s from original order for 150 F.22s (15 November 1945) by Supermarine at South Marston under contract A/C 5795/C.23(c).

Technical data – Spitfire F.24	
ENGINE	One 2,050 hp Rolls-Royce Griffon 61 RG 4SM, Griffon 64 or 85
WINGSPAN	36ft 11in
LENGTH	32ft 11in
WING AREA	244 sq/ft
LOADED WEIGHT	9,900lb
MAX SPEED	454mph at 26,000ft
RATE OF CLIMB	30,000ft in 8 mins
CEILING	43,000ft
ARMAMENT	Four 20mm Hispano cannon. One 500lb or two 250lb bombs and or RPs

Spitfire F.24 PK713 pictured at South Marston in October 1946. The Griffon 61-powered fighter was first flown by Supermarine test pilot W J G Morgan for just 20 minutes on 19 February 1946. The aircraft never joined 80 Squadron, spending much of its time at 33 MU at Lyneham before being scrapped on 2 November 1956. (Via Martyn Chorlton)

Seafire F.XV

Development

The first Seafire to be powered by the Griffon was an amalgamation of four different aircraft. The fuselage was from the Spitfire Mk V, the wing-root tanks form the Mk IX, the large fin and rudder and the retractable tail wheel from the Mk VII and the folding wings from the Seafire Mk III. Too late to see service in World War Two, the Seafire Mk XV was one of the trickiest fighters to handle, especially from an aircraft carrier, and was destined to have a short service career.

Design

The Mk XV was designed to Specification N.4/43, which effectively called for a navalised version of the Spitfire Mk VII. As mentioned earlier, the new fighter combined many good features of other marks plus a Griffon VI engine powering a 10ft 5in Rotol propeller. The big engine was cooled by a pair of large radiators under each wing; a coolant radiator under the starboard and an oil cooler and secondary radiator under the port.

The Griffon was not the ideal engine for carrier operations because of its huge amount of torque and it rotated in the opposite direction the Merlin. This meant that the Griffon-powered Seafires tended to swing towards a carrier's superstructure and this problem was not completely solved until the introduction of contra-rotating propellers. Another problem, which did not materialise until the F.XVs were at sea, was that the Griffon's supercharger clutch tended to slip at high revolutions. Once again, the problem was eventually resolved with a new clutch in early 1947.

Operational service

The first prototype was sent to the A&AEE in February 1944 for flight testing and then on to the RAE at Farnborough for catapult and arrester testing the following month. Carrier trials began in October on the HMS *Pretoria Castle* with three prototypes but all were damaged before testing could begin. The next month, the trials were attempted again, this time being more successful.

The Seafire F.XV first entered service with 802 Squadron in May 1945 and by August had embarked on HMS *Queen* for deployment in the Pacific. The mark went on to serve with the following FAA squadrons: 700, 701, 706, 709, 715, 718, 721, 728, 733, 736, 736B, 737, 751, 759, 761, 766, 767, 768, 771, 773, 777, 778, 780, 781, 787, 790, 791, 799, 800, 801, 802, 803, 804, 805, 806, 809, 883, 1831, 1832 and 1833.

The Seafire F.XV also served with the new Air Branch of the Royal Canadian Navy which was based on the carrier HMCS *Warrior*. The branch was made up of four Canadian-manned units which were transferred from the FAA; these were 803, 825, 826 and 883 Squadrons. The four squadrons were incorporated into the 18th and 19th CAG but from the summer of 1948 all began to convert to the Hawker Sea Fury.

20 de-navalised F.XVs also served with the Burmese Air Force from 1951 to 1958.

Production

Total production orders for the Seafire F.XV were placed for 790 aircraft to be built by Cunliffe-Owen and Westlands. However, only 383 F.XVs were actually built, including the six prototypes, NS487, NS490, NS493, PK240, PK243 and PK245. The prototypes were ordered on 10 March 1943 under contract Air/2901/CB.23(c) and built as Type 386 Seafire F.XV by Vickers-Armstrongs (Supermarine) under specification N.4/43.

Technical data – Seafire F.XV	
ENGINE	One 1,950hp (take-off power) Rolls-Royce Griffon VI
WINGSPAN	36ft 10in
LENGTH	32ft 3in
HEIGHT (prop vertical, tail down)	10ft 8½in
WING AREA	242 sq ft
TARE WEIGHT	6,300lb
LOADED WEIGHT	8,000lb
MAX SPEED	392mph at 36,000ft
CLIMB	20,000ft in 7 min
RATE OF CLIMB (initial)	4,000+ ft/min
RANGE	430 miles at cruising speed of 255mph
CEILING (service)	35,500ft
ARMAMENT	Four .303in machine-guns, two 20mm Hispano Mk V cannon. One 500lb bomb on the centreline, or two pairs of Mk.VIII RPs and an external centreline drop tank or 22½ gallon combat tanks

Lovely staged shot of an FAA pilot climbing aboard his Spitfire F.XV while ground crew prepare for catapulting from HMS *Illustrious*. (P A Reuter via *Aeroplane*)

Seafire F & FR.XVII

Development

A direct development of its predecessor, the prototype was a rebuild of the third Seafire F.XV NS493 with a wealth of improvements. These included a bubble canopy as standard, a cut-down rear fuselage and a stronger undercarriage and wings.

Design

The bubble hood, which was introduced on the last 30 F.XVs built, also had a curved windscreen in front of the bullet-proof section. The rear fuselage was modified to carry an additional fuel tank, which also doubled as a camera bay for a pair of F.24 cameras in the FR version.

The stronger wing gave the Mk XVII the ability to carry a pair of 250lb bombs and a pair of 22½ gallon combat tanks or eight RPs. A RATOG system could also be attached and, after the rockets had burnt for four minutes, they were jettisoned. The electrical system was also upgraded from a 12-volt to a 24-volt installation, the first time a Spitfire or Seafire had adopted it.

Another useful design change was a new long-stroke undercarriage, with a 3in longer oleo than previous marks which gave the aircraft the ability to take hard landings better and lowered the tendency to bounce. The undercarriage also allowed the American method of dropping the aircraft onto the deck, directly into the deck restraining cables.

Operational service

The Mk XVII was built to a specification that the FAA could have done with many years before and was, finally, the fighter they always wanted. The first Mk XVII was delivered to the FAA in April 1945 and entered service with 809 and 897 Squadrons following their return from the Far East. Both had disbanded by January 1946 but 807 Squadron received the new mark the previous month for service in West Germany with 2nd TAF. Only 800 Squadron really used the type operationally during 1947 and 1948 from HMS *Ocean* in the Mediterranean alongside 805 Squadron. 800 Squadron used the Mk XVII to help cover the British evacuation of Palestine. The fighter lived on in the second line with 764 Squadron until it was retired in 1954.

The Seafire F and FR.XVIII served with the following units: 701, 703, 727, 728, 736, 737, 738, 746, 759, 761, 764, 766, 778, 781, 782, 787, 799, 800, 805, 807, 809, 879, 1830, 1831, 1832 and 1833.

Production

One prototype, NS493, was converted from Seafire F.XV to Type 384, originally designated as the Seafire F.41. 20 F.XVIIs built by Cunliffe-Owen, SP323-SP327 and SP341-SP355 from an amended Seafire F.III contract.

In total, 212 were to be built by Westland in the serial range SW781 to SX546, ordered under contract Air/3853. Production ended at SX389.

Technical data – Seafire F and FR.XVII	
ENGINE	One 1,950hp Griffon VI and 26
SPAN	36ft 10in, 13ft 3in folded
LENGTH	32ft 3in
HEIGHT	10ft 8in (tail up), 13ft 6in (tail down, wings folded)
EMPTY WEIGHT	6,385lb
LOADED WEIGHT	8,148lb
MAX SPEED	387mph at 13,000ft
SERVICE CEILING	35,200ft
RATE OF CLIMB	4,600ft/ min
RANGE	435 miles
CAMERA	Two F.24 cameras, one vertical and one oblique
ARMAMENT	Two 20mm Hispano cannon and four 0.303in Browning machine guns
BOMB-LOAD	One 250lb or 500lb bomb under fuselage and one 250lb bomb or eight 60lb rockets under each wing

Right: The prototype F.XVII, NS493, which was originally the third production Seafire XV. The fighter spent time with the RAE and 787 Squadron at West Raynham before being SOC in June 1946. (Via Martyn Chorlton)

Below: F.XVII while briefly on the strength of 767 Squadron at Yeovilton in 1949. The fighter ended its days cocooned at Stretton in 1955 and was SOC the following year. (Via Martyn Chorlton)

Seafire F & FR.45

Development

The next mark of Seafire came about because of the Spitfire F.21, which had not escaped the attentions of the Admiralty. A navalised version was requested with the same excellent performance. Specification N.7/44 was issued, and the number Mk 45 was allocated to the new Seafire with work being carried out by Cunliffe-Owen. As in all previous cases, Supermarine still retained the design authority.

Design

The Seafire F.45 was the first of the breed to take advantage of the 2,035hp Griffon 60 series engine which would give the fighter a maximum speed of 442mph; considerably faster than previous marks. The first aircraft, TM379 (ex-F.21 LA193), was fitted with a 'sting-type' arrestor hook, which made it the longest Spitfire/Seafire yet at 33ft 4in. It was fitted with standard F.21 wings without folding joints, relegating the mark to operations from shore bases only. Fuel capacity was 120 gallons spread across two main fuselage tanks at the front, a lower tank, an upper tank and a pair built into the leading edges of the wings. Armament was four 20mm Hispano cannons.

The aircraft suffered from the same swing issues as the Mk XVII, which was another reason for avoiding carrier operations, although trials would later take place on HMS *Pretoria Castle*. The problem of swing was tested on TM379, fitted with a contra-rotating propeller on 10 April 1945. Two other F.45 prototypes, LA442 and LA444, were fitted with a Griffon 85 engine and a contra-rotating propeller that would lead to the Seafire F.46. A few F.45s were fitted with this combination of propeller and engine.

The F.45 had the benefit of a larger-chord rudder and bigger elevators, which made the mark much easier to handle than the Seafire Mk XV and the Spitfire F.21.

Operational service

Trials were extensive before the F.45 entered service, including sea trials on HMS *Pretoria Castle*, despite being of little value on board an aircraft carrier. TM379, LA440, LA441 and LA480 carried out 239 landings on the carrier and only suffered two undercarriage failures during the sea trial. LA494 managed to reach Mach 0.88 (580.8mph) during diving trials making it the fastest propeller-driven aircraft to serve with the Royal Navy.

The F.45 first entered service with 778 Squadron at Ford in June 1945 followed by 700, 703, 709, 771, 777, 780 and 787 Squadrons, all second line units. A few of the 50 F.45s built were converted to FR.45s from March 1947 with a pair of F.24 cameras in the rear fuselage. The last F.45s continued to serve until September 1950 when they were retired from 771 Squadron at Arbroath.

Production

50 F.45s in the serial range, LA428-LA457 and LA480-LA499 were built at South Marston and ordered under contract B.981687/39 and Ctts/Acft/1952 from Vickers-Armstrong. The prototype, TM379, ex-Spitfire F.21 was ordered from Castle Bromwich under contract Air/4425/C.23(c) (7 May 1944).

An order for 600 further aircraft, VD490-VE593, ordered under contract Air/4424/C.23(c) was cancelled on 1 August 1945.

Technical data – Seafire F.45	
ENGINE	One 2,035hp (at 7,000ft) Rolls-Royce Griffon 61
WINGSPAN	36ft 11in
LENGTH	33ft 4in
HEIGHT (tail up)	12ft
WING AREA	242 sq ft
OVERLOAD WEIGHT	11,250lb
MAX SPEED	442mph
CLIMB RATE	4,800 ft/min
CEILING (service)	41,500ft
ARMAMENT	Four 20mm Hispano Mk II or Mk V cannon. One 500lb bomb under fuselage or a pair of 250lb bombs under each wing

Right: The prototype F.45, TM379, was originally LA193 but was taken from the production line to be converted by Cunliffe-Owen under Specification N.7/44. First flown on 31 August 1944, TM379 was one of the most heavily tested and trialled prototypes ever built by Supermarine. (Via Martyn Chorlton)

Below: Two F.45s were fitted with the Griffon 85 engine, a five blade contra-rotating propeller. This is one of them, LA442, pictured during trials in the new configuration in late 1945 with Sqn Ldr Womack at the controls. Transferred to the RAE in 1950, the fighter was also involved in special rocket catapult trials, along with LA439 and LA450. (Via Martyn Chorlton)

Seafire F.46

Development

The penultimate mark of the long Spitfire/Seafire lineage was the F.46, which was based on the Spitfire F.22, complete with chopped down rear fuselage and bubble canopy. Described as the first Griffon-powered Seafire able to operate from an aircraft carrier safely, the F.46 was given little chance to perform, as only 24 were built, whereas its younger sibling, the F.47, would.

Design

The F.46, first obvious feature was that the contra-rotating propeller was fitted as standard, making the fighter much easier to handle, especially when taking off from an aircraft carrier. This was a particularly useful feature as power was increased again with the Griffon 87 (production aircraft). The fin and rudder was also increased in size to counteract the increased forward side area created by the double propeller and longer spinner. The area of the tailplane and the elevators was also increased and all but the early production aircraft were built with the same, bigger, Spiteful tail units.

Like the F.45, the wing could not fold but the electrical system was upgraded to a 24 volt installation and the fuel system was changed to accommodate an additional 32-gallon fuel tank in the rear fuselage. Also, 22½ gallon drop tanks could be carried under the wing and a single 50 gallon tank under the fuselage.

LA545 was the only F.46 to be fitted with the Griffon 88 engine with fuel injection, replacing the Bendix-Stromberg induction-injection carburettor that was fitted to earlier engines. LA545 also trialled an improved air-intake filter, which was brought forward to just under the propeller. Both the engine and intake would feature in the forthcoming F.47.

Operational service

As with the F.45, the initial conversion work of the prototype, TM383, powered by a Griffon 86, was carried out by Cunliffe-Owen. TM383 first flew on 8 September 1944 with a Griffon 61 engine. The first of 24 production aircraft, LA541, all built by Vickers-Armstrongs at South Marston, first flew in October 1945 but did not enter service until the following year with 736 Squadron at St Merryn. Despite so few being built, the F and FR.45 managed to serve with the following units, 736, 738, 767, 771, 777, 778, 781, 787 and 1832 Squadrons until mid-1950. The type also appeared at RNAS Anthorn and three were allocated to the Empire Test Pilots School at Cranfield.

Production

In total 24 F.46s, LA541-LA564, were built at by Vickers-Armstrongs, South Marston, under contract Air/5794/CB.23(c) (B981687/39).

Technical data – Spitfire F.46	
ENGINE	One 2,300hp Rolls-Royce Griffon 86 (Prototype), 87 (Production aircraft) and 88 (LA545 only)
WINGSPAN	36ft 11in
LENGTH	33ft 7in
HEIGHT (prop vertical, tail down)	12ft 6in
WING AREA	244 sq ft
TARE WEIGHT	7,100lb
LOADED WEIGHT	9,400lb
MAX SPEED	443mph at 25,000ft
CLIMB	20,000ft in 7.4 min
RATE OF CLIMB (initial)	3,750 ft/min
RANGE	435 miles at cruising speed of 272mph
CEILING (service)	41,000ft
ARMAMENT	Four 20mm Hispano cannon

Seafire F.46, LA542, the second of only 24 production aircraft built. The fighter was briefly used for combat tank and 9.5in RP trials from South Marston before being relegated to storage at 39 MU at Colerne. (Via Martyn Chorlton)

Seafang

Development

During October 1943, Supermarine had the foresight to see that the laminar flow wing that was being applied to the Spiteful project could also be used on the Seafire Mk XV. This naval variant was created under Supermarine's own specification number 474, was given the designation Type 382 and was to be fitted with the Merlin 61 engine.

Eventually, the Royal Navy began to show an interest in a laminar flow Seafire and the specification N.5/45 for such a fighter was issued.

Design

Rather than building an aircraft from scratch, Spiteful F.14 RB520 was modified to become the first prototype Seafang in early 1945. RB520 was fitted with a 'sting-type' arrestor hook and was only referred to as an interim Seafang prototype.

A pair of Type 396 Seafang Mk 32 prototypes were ordered in March 1945 to be followed by a healthy order for 150 Type 382 Seafang Mk 31s in May 1945. These aircraft would basically be the same as RB520, which was nothing more than a navalised Spiteful. The theory was that the fully equipped Spiteful, the Mk 32, could be developed while the interim Mk 31s were in service. Regardless, the end of the war intervened and only nine of the 150 Mk 31s ordered were ever built.

The first 'proper' Seafang prototype, Mk 32 VB895, was first flown by Mike Lithgow in June 1946. Powered by a 2,350hp Griffon 89 engine, the fighter was also fitted with hydraulically operated folding wings and a three-blade contra-rotating propeller.

Operational service

Lithgow carried out a host of trials in VB895 including deck-landing and simulated landings at RNAS and Chilbolton. The results proved that the Seafang was more than suitable for deck operations, giving a good pilot's view of the deck and an approach speed of 95 kt. The Spiteful did not float when the throttle was closed either.

Lithgow demonstrated VB895 to the Dutch navy in August 1946 and carried out deck landing trials on HMS *Illustrious* in May 1947. Neither the Dutch nor the Royal Navy would order the Seafang, the latter seeing no significant improvement over the aircraft that it was meant to replace, the Seafire F.47. Despite earlier tests, the low speed handling of the Seafang was not as good as the Sea Fury, which was retained as the FAA's last piston-engined fighter.

In the end, the Seafang's contribution to aircraft development was greater than realised at the time and one aircraft, Mk 31 VG474, played a useful role in the creation of a new era of FAA aircraft, in the shape of the Attacker. Both the Spiteful and the Seafang had helped to create the next major Supermarine product straight from the drawing board.

Production

Only 18 Seafangs were built out of the 153 ordered because the vast majority of them were cancelled at the end of World War Two. One prototype, RT646, was cancelled while the two prototypes, ordered to specification N.5/45, were built under contract Air/5176 (21 April 1945).

Out of the batch of 150, only 16 Seafang F.31s and F.32s were built.

Technical data – Type 382 Seafang F.32	
ENGINE	One 2,350hp Rolls-Royce Griffon 89
WINGSPAN	35ft
LENGTH	34ft 1in
HEIGHT	12ft 6½in
WING AREA	210 sq ft
TARE WEIGHT	8,000lb
LOADED WEIGHT	10,450lb
MAX SPEED	475mph at 21,000ft
RATE OF CLIMB (initial)	4,630 ft/min
RANGE	393 miles at 220–240mph
CEILING (service)	41,000ft
ARMAMENT	Four 20mm Hispano cannon with 624 rounds and provision for two 1,000lb or four 300lb RPs, a pair under each wing

Supermarine Seafang Mk 32 VB895 which was first flown by Mike Lithgow in June 1946.

Seafire F & F.47

Development

The Seafire F.47 marked the finale to the entire Spitfire story, which really began in action during the Battle of Britain in 1940 and was destined to end in action over Korea in 1950. The F.47 represented the pinnacle of Spitfire's development and it was certainly the best of all the Seafires.

Design

The Seafire F.47 was designed to meet another Royal Navy requirement, which was for folding wings. These were a completely new design and were hinged outside of the cannon bay. Being further out when folded, the wing tips were at a height of 13ft 10in, which meant that the wing tips did not need to fold as well. The first four off the production line were manually folded while the rest were hydraulically powered.

The F.47's wing was much stronger than the F.46, giving it the ability to carry a 500lb bomb under each of eight 60lb RPs or a pair of 22½ gallon fuel tanks. With reference to the latter, the F.47 was quite a 'bowser' with extra leading edge tanks, rear fuselage tanks, combat tanks and the provision for a 90-gallon drop tank under the fuselage giving the fighter a potential range of over a 1,000 miles. Even when fully loaded, the F.47 could still manage 433mph at 24,000ft and when running light could reach 452mph.

Operational service

The F.47 did not enter service until January 1948 with 804 Squadron who were based at Ford. By 1949, HMS *Triumph* was carrying the only Seafire squadron still at sea, namely 800 Squadron, flying the FR.47. Serving with the Far East Fleet, the carrier was part of the 13th CAG when it disembarked 800 Squadron at Sembawang to join the fighting against communist guerrillas in Malaya. Action began on 21 October when ten Seafires attacked a guerrilla position with rockets. Further raids were flown until the squadron re-embarked on Triumph on 1 November for the voyage to Hong Kong.

After visiting Japan, HMS *Triumph* had just set sail for Hong Kong on 24 June 1950 when news came through of the North Korean invasion. On 3 July, the task force was in position off the Korean coast. Within hours, *Triumph* launched its first attack made up of 12 Seafires and nine Fireflies firing rockets at Heju airfield. The following day, Seafires were sent up to attack targets of opportunity, only for the British element of the task force to leave for Sasebo and Okinawa to refuel and replenish on 5 July. During their brief stay at Okinawa, the Seafires had 'D-Day' style invasion stripes painted on them purely to help the Americans distinguish them from the enemy Yak-9s.

On 13 September, HMS *Triumph* prepared to support more landings, this time at Inchon. By 20 September, *Triumph* had four serviceable Seafires on board, with no replacements in sight. Out of these four, only one was allowed to fly combat operations and it was clear that neither *Triumph* nor the Seafire could continue. On 21 September 1950, HMS *Triumph* returned to Sasebo bringing to an end the operational career of the Seafire.

Production

The F.47 was built in three production batches, the first was for 14 aircraft (PS944 to PS957), the second for 64 (VP427 to VP465 and VP471 to VP495) and the third for 12 aircraft (VR961 to VR972), all built by Vickers Armstrongs at South Marston.

Technical data – Type 382 Seafire F.47	
ENGINE	2,145hp Rolls-Royce Griffon 87 or 2,350hp Griffon 88
WINGSPAN	36ft 11in; (folded) 25ft 5in
LENGTH	34ft 6in (to tip of arrestor hook)
HEIGHT	12ft 6in (tail down)
EMPTY WEIGHT	7,625lb
LOADED WEIGHT	10,200lb
MAX WEIGHT	12,750lb
MAX SPEED	452mph at 20,500ft or 433mph at 24,000ft
RATE OF CLIMB	4,800ft/min
SERVICE CEILING	43,100ft
RANGE	405 miles plus 15 mins combat. Over 1,000 miles with full fuel load
ARMAMENT	Four 20mm British Hispano Mk V cannon. Bomb-load: Two 500lb or 250lb bombs or eight 60lb rockets or one Mk IX depth charge

Right: The first of 90 Seafire F.47s built was the Griffon 87 powered PS944, which first flew on 25 April 1946 in the hands of Supermarine test pilot Dave Morgan. (Via Martyn Chorlton)

Below: A Seafire F.47 fully tooled up at Boscombe Down with a pair of 500lb bombs, under wing combat tanks and a 90-gallon drop tank under the fuselage. (Via Martyn Chorlton)

Attacker F.1, FB.1 & FB.2

Development

In March 1944, Rolls-Royce began to design a new turbojet that could produce twice the power of its own Derwent, which was being produced in mass for Gloster Meteor. Capable of producing 4,000lb static thrust, the engine was designated as the RB.40. Not long after, Supermarine was asked to design a new fighter to Specification E.1/44 around the new RB.40 engine. Chief Designer Joe Smith actually wanted a smaller engine for the design, which was originally called the 'Spiteful development'. The smaller 3,000lb static thrust engine was redesignated the RB.41 and later to be known as the Nene and Smith's 'Jet Spiteful' then would become the Attacker.

Design

Work on the drawings for the Attacker began only a week before the first flight of the Spiteful. The significance of this was that the Attacker was being designed with a laminar flow wing, which was yet to be fully tested and is where the Spiteful would play its part.

In a short period of time, the design of the new jet, under Supermarine specification 477, was presented to the DTD (Director of Technical Development) featuring the RB.41 engine, laminar flow wings with radiators removed and replaced with fuel tanks, a pressurised cockpit and 20mm cannon. On 5 August 1944, three prototypes, TS409, TS413 and TS416 were ordered by the Air Ministry as 'jet machines of the Spiteful type'.

By October 1944, trials began of the RB.41, which initially proved disappointing but, once intake swirl vanes were introduced, the engine surpassed original estimates by achieving 4,500lb of thrust at 12,000rpm.

Development of the Spiteful was to be slower than expected, marred by the loss of the second prototype. However, an order for 24 aircraft, six of them to the original E.10/44 specification and 18 to E.1/45 for the Royal Navy, were ordered in July 1945. Unfortunately, this order was 'pigeon-holed' because of the handling difficulties that had been experienced during the Spiteful trials. Work on the three original prototypes did continue though despite this.

Operational history

The first prototype, TS409, made its maiden flight in the hands of Jeffrey Quill on 27 July 1946. The Attacker was the first individual aircraft to be fitted with the Nene engine and also the first true prototype of a brand new design to flight-tested at Boscombe Down. Following trials with the A&AEE, TS409, made its public debut at the SBAC at Radlett in September 1946.

The second prototype, TS413, was modified to Admiralty Specification E.1/45 and was called the Attacker F.1. The jet was first flown by Mike Lithgow on 17 June 1947, but it was not until November 1949 that firm orders were placed by the FAA. The F.1, with its four 20mm Hispano Mk V cannon and Nene Mk 101 engine, first entered service with 800 Squadron on 17 August 1951. Two other variants followed, both seeing service with the FAA; the FB.1 had a strengthened wing with hard points for bombs or RPs and the FB.2 was the same but fitted with a Nene 102.

The Attacker enjoyed only a brief period of service with the FAA which saw it withdrawn from all operational squadrons by 1954, replaced by the Hawker Sea Hawk and de Havilland Venom. The Attacker served with the following squadrons: (F.1) 702, 703, 736, 767, 787, 800, 803 and 890; (FB.1) 703, 767, 787, 800 and 890; (FB.2) 700, 703, 718, 736, 767, 787, 800, 803, 890, 1831, 1832 and 1833 Squadrons.

Production

FAA Three prototypes, TS409, TS413 and TS416 were ordered as Type 392 under contract Air/4562/CB.7(b) (9 September 1944) to specification E.10/44. First production aircraft, WA469-WA537 (63) were ordered in November 1949 to specification 1/45/PI/SU and contract 6/Air/2822/CB.7(b). WA469-WA498 and WA505-WA526 as F.1s; WA527-WA534 as FB.1s. WK319-WK342 (24) ordered as FB.2s. WP275-WP303 (30) ordered as FB.2s. WT851 a FB.1. WZ273-WZ302 (30) as FB.2s.

Pakistan: R4000-R4035 (36), Type 538 (land-based) built for Pakistan Air Force.

Technical data – Attacker F.1	
ENGINE	One 5,000lb st Rolls-Royce Nene 3 or (FB.2) Nene 102
WINGSPAN	36ft 11in. (folded) 28ft 11in
LENGTH (tail down)	37ft 1in
HEIGHT (tail down)	9ft 6½in
WING AREA	227.2 sq ft
SWEEPBACK (outboard of kink)	2.7°. (inboard): 1.7°
TARE WEIGHT	8,426lb
LOADED WEIGHT	12,211lb
MAX SPEED	590mph at sea level
RATE OF CLIMB (maximum)	6,350 ft/min
CLIMB (to 30,000ft)	6.6 min
RANGE (maximum with overload tank)	1,190 miles at 355mph
CEILING (service)	45,000ft
ARMAMENT	Four 20mm Hispano Mk V cannon with 624 rounds in wings, and two 1,000lb or four 300lb RPs under the wings

Above left: First delivered to the Royal Navy on 1 August 1951, Attacker F.1, WA497, saw service with 890 and 736 Squadron before being written off aboard HMS *Eagle* on 14 September 1952. (*Aeroplane*)

Above right: The prototype Type 392 Attacker TS409 pictured not long after its first flight on 27 July 1946. By February 1953 the aircraft was withdrawn from use but served on as RNAS Instructional Airframe A2313 at Arbroath until it was scrapped in 1956. (Via Martyn Chorlton)

Seagull ASR Mk 1

Development

The Seagull ASR Mk I marked the last of many amphibian flying boats designed by Supermarine from the First World War. The design was originally put forward for Air Ministry Specification S.12/40 in 1940 for a fleet amphibian capable of being stowed on a warship. Following the success of the Walrus and Sea Otter, Supermarine seemed well placed to develop the idea further. Little did the company know that it would take eight years before the final Seagull took flight.

Design

The all-metal Seagull had a twin spar parasol wing mounted on a large pylon that joined the fuselage. Originally designed for a Merlin engine, as time passed by, the more powerful Griffon became available. This was tractor mounted on top of the central pylon, driving a contra-rotating propeller. The pylon was so big that the rear part of it was made into an observer's position with two large windows either side.

The wing was a complicated affair, fitted with slotted flaps and leading edge slats that ran the full length and could fold for stowage onboard ship. The wing also incorporated technology that had already been tried and tested with the Type 322 'Dumbo', i.e., the variable-incidence wing. The wing's incidence could be changed by pivoting at the forward spar and was controlled by a jackscrew that was electrically driven and fitted the rear spar.

The hull was a standard longeron design while the tailplane was an impressive-looking creation with a high dihedral with three fins. The undercarriage neatly retracted into wells on each side of the fuselage and, when used as a flying boat, it could be removed, making the Seagull 400lb lighter. An arrestor hook and mounts for RATOG were also fitted.

Service

Three prototypes, PA143, PA147 and PA152, were originally ordered on 9 April 1943 but it was not until 14 July 1948 that the first aircraft flew for the first time from Itchen in the hands of Lt Cdr Mike Lithgow. Some of the many reasons for the aircraft's protracted development was the relocation of the Supermarine design office, the lack of wind-tunnel testing available, a change of engine and, most significantly, a change of specification. The new requirement that appeared in 1944 was S.14/44, which changed the Seagull into an air-sea rescue and reconnaissance flying boat, discarding any need for armament which was to include a four-gun turret.

The second prototype, PA147, was in the air by September 1949 and it was this aircraft that carried out proving trials on board HMS *Ark Royal* followed by deck landing on HMS *Illustrious*. Initial handling problems were eventually ironed out and the variable-incidence wing proved its worth when Lithgow demonstrated the Seagull's slow speed qualities by managing to remain airborne at just 35mph! In contrast, test pilot Les R Colquhoun gained the World's Air Speed for amphibians over 100 kilometres during the Air League Cup Race at Sherburn-in-Elmet in PA147 at an average speed of 241.9mph.

Unfortunately, the age of the flying boat was well and truly over and, by the early 1950s, helicopters could carry out the air-sea rescue role. Only two of the three planned Seagulls were completed, the third, PA152, was only part built and by 1952 all had been scrapped.

Production

Three prototypes, PA143, PA147 and PA152, were ordered 9 April 1943 under contract Air/2964/CB.20(b) to specification S.12/40. PA152 was not built.

Technical data – Seagull ASR Mk 1	
ENGINE	One 1,815hp Rolls-Royce 29
WINGSPAN	52ft 6in
WIDTH (max with wing folded)	23ft 6in
LENGTH	44ft 1½in
HEIGHT (tail down)	15ft 10½in
WING AREA	432 sq ft
EMPTY WEIGHT	10,510lb
LOADED WEIGHT	14,500lb

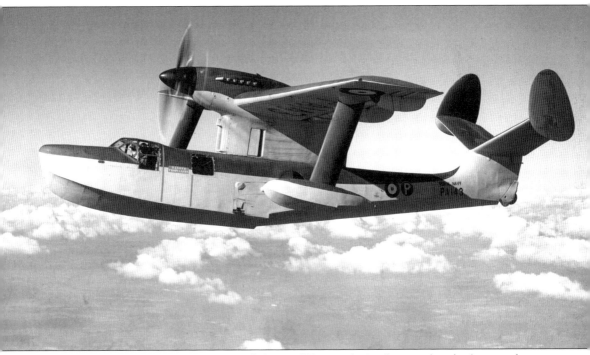

The Seagull ASR Mk I was a good-looking aircraft that would have undoubtedly entered production as early as 1942 if Supermarine's circumstances had been different. This is the first prototype, PA143, during early flight testing with the original twin fin tailplane arrangement. (*Aeroplane*)

PA147 was first flown on 2 September 1949 and, just 13 days later, appeared at the SBAC show, Farnborough. The aircraft featured the final tailplane arrangement with a taller centre fin and is pictured arriving at Farnborough. (Via Martyn Chorlton)

Type 510/517 'Swift'

Development

In 1946, the Air Staff issued specifications for new heavy bombers and two-seat and single-seater fighters. One of the latter was a development of the Attacker, with swept wings, under the designation E.41/46 designed to replace the Gloster Meteor.

Supermarine won a contract to produce two prototypes under the latest specification, the first of which was given the serial VV106.

Design

Built at Hursley Park, VV106 had the fuselage of an Attacker but was fitted with 40° swept-back wings and tailplanes. Power was provided by a single Rolls-Royce Nene 2 engine and design speed, at first, was limited to 700mph.

At first, the aircraft had a rounded nose and the pitot tube fitted to the port wing tip. However, during early development, the nose was modified with a pronounced point, which increased speed and the pitot tube was also moved to the extreme nose.

Operational service

The Type 510 VV106 was first flown by Mike Lithgow from Boscombe Down on 29 December 1948. It had unwittingly become Britain's first jet-engined aircraft to fly with both swept wings and tailplanes. Lithgow was suitably impressed with the new aircraft and within a few flights was comfortably reaching Mach 0.9 without drama.

Demonstrated at the 1949 SBAC show in September, it was then passed to the A&AEE at Boscombe Down for handling trials. It was here that advantages and disadvantages of the design were revealed. While the sweepback improved high Mach characteristics, the design also introduced longitudinal instability just before the stall, limiting manoeuvrability at high altitude. For example, at 40,000ft the Type 510, now referred to as the Swift, was virtually limited to straight flight only. At lower levels, the aircraft was viceless and the excellent ailerons gave a good rate of roll, a good sign that the Type 510 had the potential to become a good fighter.

In July 1950, the RAE carried out a comparison with the F-86A Sabre. The American jet was a better performer by far at low level but at 25,000ft the two aircraft put in very similar figures, with the type 510 achieving 617mph and the Sabre 619.5mph.

By late 1950, the Type 510 was adapted for FAA deck landing trials and, on 20 September, was delivered to Farnborough for dummy deck-landing tests. On 8 November 1950 the Type 510 achieved another first by becoming the first swept-wing jet to land and take off from an aircraft carrier. This historic flight was carried out by Lt J Elliot RN on HMS *Illustrious*.

Back in December 1948, Supermarine had come up with its own specification 515 stating that the Swift, with its swept-wings, should be capable of breaching Mach 1. To achieve this, and to maintain control it was decided that an adjustable tailplane should be fitted as well as a host of more subtle modifications. VV106 was suitably modified and was redesignated Type 517.

The whole of the rear-fuselage could now be adjusted through the vertical plane by 4° in either direction giving the Type 517 a very effective trimmer. Initially limited to Mach 0.95, this was soon relaxed and those pilots who flew the fighter in its new guise commented favourably.

Production

A single aircraft was built to specification E.41/46 under contract 6/Acft/1031 (13 March 1946) and given the serial VV106.

Technical data – Type 510 (E.41/46)	
ENGINE	One Rolls-Royce Nene 2
WINGSPAN	32ft 8in
LENGTH	38ft 1in
HEIGHT	9ft 10in
WING AREA	272.96 sq ft
TAKE-OFF WEIGHT	12,200lb
MAX SPEED	630–645mph at 10,000ft

The only Type 510 VV106 pictured off the Needles, Isle of Wight circa 1949. (Via Martyn Chorlton)

Type 528/535

Development

The Type 528 was the second of two Supermarine prototypes which came about because of Specification E.41/46. Despite the different Supermarine designation, the aircraft differed little from the Type 510 and was registered as VV119.

Design

As with the Type 510, the Type 528 relied heavily on the Attacker for its fuselage and was fitted with a set of 40° swept wings and tailplanes. The aircraft was to exist in the guise for only a short period after its first flight in March 1950. By May, the aircraft was grounded for a variety of modifications, which transformed into the Type 535.

Changes included fitting a tricycle undercarriage, a larger rear fuselage for a bigger jet-pipe and reheated engine, a new tail cone to reduce the diameter to keep the fuselage aerodynamic, bigger air-intakes, provision for guns in the wings, shorter ailerons, a redesigned cockpit canopy, removal of anti-spin parachute, which dispensed with the need for a housing behind the rudder, a longer nose, an improved fuel system and finally, larger fuel tanks raising capacity to 400 gallons.

The centre-section of the wing was also made larger by reducing the sweep of the trailing edge. The sum of the modifications made the Type 535 4ft longer than the original aircraft.

Operational service

The original Type 528, VV119, was first flown by Mike Lithgow from Boscombe Down on 27 March 1950. In the guise of the Type 535, VV119 first flew from Boscombe Down again on 23 August 1950 and by 1 September was operating with reheat. A few days later, the more refined Type 535, with many of the foibles of the Type 510 now removed, was performing at the SBAC display at Farnborough.

While testing continued, Supermarine was encouraged to continue with the Swift development when an order for 100 production aircraft was placed in November 1950. VV119 continued to provide very useful service during this period and even starred in the film *Sound Barrier* in 1951, which was a first for a working prototype.

VV119 continued to be used for test flying until 1955 but by September this very useful aircraft was reduced to a ground instructional airframe and donated to No.1 SoTT at RAF Halton.

Production

A single aircraft built to specification E.41/46 under contract 6/Acft/1031 (13 March 1946) and given the serial VV119.

Technical data – Type 528/535 (E.41/46)	
ENGINE	(528) Rolls-Royce Nene 3, later afterburning variant
WINGSPAN	32ft 8in
LENGTH	(528) 38ft 1in (535) 42ft 1in
HEIGHT	9ft 10in
WING AREA	272.96 sq ft
TAKE-OFF WEIGHT	12,200lb
SPEED (level flight)	622mph at 15,000ft, 609mph at 26,000ft and 583mph at 35,000ft

Swift VV119 with test pilot Dave Morgan at the controls during filming of the Sound Barrier in 1951. (Via Martyn Chorlton)

Type 541 Swift

Development

The Type 541s came about as part of a 100-strong Swift F.1 production order in November 1950, which also called for a pair of pre-production prototypes. The first, WJ960, differed very little from the Type 535 VV119, while the second Type 541, WJ965, took another step closer to how the production Swift F.1 would finally appear.

Design

The only subtle difference between the Type 541 and the Type 535 was that the ailerons on WJ960 were slightly longer because of the lack of space provided for wing-mounted guns. WJ965, the second pre-production Type 541, was a different looking machine, with a modified nose, canopy and fin. The wing was also in a slightly different position, in relation to the fuselage, and the wing-tips were a Kuchemann curved design, which also featured on WJ960. WJ965's internal fuel capacity was also greater.

Both Type 541s were powered by the Rolls-Royce AJ.65 turbojet, which was narrower than the earlier Nene. Despite the size difference, neither aircraft was redesigned for the slimmer engine but the production models were.

Operational service

WJ960 was first flown by Mike Lithgow from Boscombe Down on 1 August 1950. Lithgow's early experiences with the Type 541 were not pleasant ones as a variety of control oscillations occurred. On his third flight, two days later, control vibrations were so severe a fuel cock linkage broke forcing Lithgow to make a dead-stick landing into Chilbolton without damage to the aircraft.

Supermarine test pilot Dave Morgan had a similar experience whilst practicing for the 1951 SBAC in WJ960. Morgan suffered an engine failure but like Lithgow before him, managed to carry out a good forced landing at Chilbolton with only minimal, repairable damage to the aircraft.

WJ960 was later fitted with a variable-incidence tail and, on 4 February 1953, the aircraft managed to reach Mach 0.91 but aileron flutter brought to an end any ideas of getting close to the sound barrier.

WJ965, the second pre-production aircraft, was first flown by Dave Morgan from Boscombe Down on 18 July 1952. This aircraft was more in line with how the production Swift F.1 would appear and as a result incorporated considerably more 'operational' features than WJ960.

After further modifications some, including the replacement of the aircraft aileron spring-tab with geared tabs, were brought about by the DH.110's fatal crash at the SBAC in 1952. In its final form, WJ965 became the first Supermarine aircraft to exceed Mach 1 in a dive on 26 February 1953.

Production

WJ960 and WJ965. Two pre-production aircraft, WJ960 and WJ965, built to specification F105 under contract 6/Acft/5986 (November 1950) as Type 541.

Technical data – Type 541	
ENGINE	One 7,500lb Rolls-Royce (A.J.65) Avon
WINGSPAN	32ft 8in
LENGTH	(528) 38ft 1in (535) 42ft 1in
HEIGHT	9ft 10in
WING AREA	272.96 sq ft
TAKE-OFF WEIGHT	12,200lb
SPEED (level flight)	622mph at 15,000ft, 609mph at 26,000ft and 583mph at 35,000ft

Right: The second pre-production Swift WJ965 being flown by Dave Morgan and pictured over Salisbury Plain during early flight trials from Boscombe Down in 1952. (Via Martyn Chorlton)

Below: No finer study of the first Type 545, WJ960 by renowned aviation photographer Charles E. Brown. (Charles E. Brown via Martyn Chorlton)

Type 505/508 & 525

Development

The story of the early development of what was to become the last of the aircraft solely designed by the Supermarine division of Vickers-Armstrongs (Aircraft) began in 1945. What was to become the Scimitar began as a remit from the Admiralty for an aircraft without an undercarriage and which could be catapulted from the deck of a carrier and recovered on a landing 'carpet'. The lack of an undercarriage would save weight and drag and, despite the concept being very novel, the ten years of development involved still resulted in a conventional, albeit very technical, aircraft.

History

By 1947, the idea of an aircraft without an undercarriage began to lose favour with the Admiralty and, in quick response, Supermarine redesignated the Type 505 to the Type 508 incorporating a retractable three-wheel undercarriage. Increased dimensions across the board changed the performance figures, generally for the better, and included a lower landing speed. Because of the undercarriage, a slightly thicker wing did no harm, improving low-level performance and general landing characteristics. Internally, the main difference between the 505 and 508 was that the latter had its main wing spars running under the fuselage so as to provide anchor positions for the undercarriage.

In the background, Supermarine had successfully tested and flown a swept wing version of the Attacker which itself was developed into the Type 541 Swift Mk I. The same was applied to the Type 508 and a new swept wing version heralded the Type 525. To compensate for the new geometry, a taller undercarriage was fitted further out, which, in turn, increased the width of the aircraft with the wings folded. NACA double-slotted flaps that extended under the fuselage, as well as tapered nose flaps along the leading edge of wing, helped the Type 525 reach the operational criteria required for high-speed carrier landings.

The original 'butterfly' was at first left in place, although it was slightly swept back. However, structural problems began to creep in and the Type 525's tail was replaced by a traditional crucifix design. Only minor modifications were needed to fit the two Avon engines, although fuel capacity was increased. The result was that the draft specification N.113D and a contract was placed for two prototypes which grew into three. The Type 508, VX133 was first flown in 1951 from Boscombe Down followed by development of the Type 525, the Type 529. This had cannons installed, an extended tail cone and strakes in front of the fins and, as VX136, first flew August 1952. The prototype, Type 525, on which the Scimitar would be based, first flew in April 1954.

Production

Three aircraft VX133 (Type 508), VX136 (Type 529) and VX138 (Type 525) were ordered under specification N.9/47 and contract 6/Air/1508/CB.7. By October 1950, the contract changed to 6/Air/5772/CB.7 with VX138 fitted with swept-back wings.

Technical data – Type 529	
ENGINE	Two 6,500lb Rolls-Royce Avon RA.3
WINGSPAN	41ft
LENGTH	(525) 52ft. (529) 50ft
HEIGHT	12ft 7in
WING AREA	(505) 270 sq ft. (508) 310 sq ft. (529) 340.03 sq ft
EMPTY WEIGHT	18,459lb
MAX SPEED	607mph
ARMAMENT	Provision for four 20mm cannon.

Above: Type 529 VX136 during deck handling and flight trials on board HMS *Eagle* on 5 November 1953. (Via Martyn Chorlton)

Right: The prototype Type 525 VX138 at Boscombe Down, just prior to its maiden flight on 27 April 1954. (Via Martyn Chorlton)

Swift F.1

Development

The Swift F.1 had come about from a decision made back in 1951 by the Prime Minister Sir Winston Churchill for 'super-priority' production. The decision had been made in response to world affairs of the day including increasing tension between NATO and the Warsaw Pact and the Korean War, which had begun the previous year.

The resulting development work had seen the Type 510, 517, 528, 535 and the Type 541 Swift all make in-roads into giving the RAF its first swept wing fighter jet. Unfortunately, the Swift F.1 would prove to be one of the biggest post-war anti-climaxes and was destined to play no part in the Korean War, nor any significant role within NATO.

Design

A preliminary order for just 18 Swift F.1s was placed, the first, WK194, first flew on 25 August 1952. WK194 and WK195 differed very little from the pre-production Type 541 but, from WK196 onwards, first flown in March 1953, the first proper production was born. WK194 and WK195 were handmade in the Hursley Park experimental shops. WK196 onwards and all subsequent Swifts went through the final assembly stages at South Marston.

All production Swift F.1s were fitted with fully-boosted controls but before the aircraft even entered service there was an Air Ministry request to upgrade the two 30mm Aden cannons to a set of four. With production already underway, the modification was not deemed worthwhile and in hindsight was irrelevant because production of the F.1 was brought to a close after the preliminary order was completed.

Operational service

The Swift F.1 first entered service with 56 Squadron at Waterbeach on 13 February 1954. The occasion was somewhat dumbed down by the fact that the RAF's latest jet fighter had a collection of flight restrictions applied to it. These included a limited maximum speed, a reduced service ceiling and the guns only being fired in unrealistic straight and level attitude, rendering the Swift F.1 non-operational. Engine failures were a very common occurrence and, despite all of the Swift's foibles being officially written off as teethingproblems, the F.1 was grounded in August 1954.

Further restrictions were applied and 56 Squadron struggled on with a handful Swift F.1s until March 1955 when it reverted to its original Meteor F.8s.

Production

18 production aircraft to specification F105P under contract 6/Acft/5969/CB.5(b) (November 1950). Aircraft were in the following serial ranges; WK194-WK197 and WK200-WK213.

Technical data – Swift F.1	
ENGINE	One Rolls-Royce Avon RA.3/105.
WINGSPAN	32.35ft
LENGTH	41ft ½in
HEIGHT	13ft ½in
WING AREA	306.2 sq ft
TARE WEIGHT	11,892lb
LOADED WEIGHT	15,800lb
MAX SPEED	660mph at sea level
CLIMB	40,000ft in 5.16 min
RANGE	730 miles
RATE OF CLIMB	12,300 ft/min
CEILING	45,500ft
ARMAMENT	Two 30mm Aden cannon

The first production Swift F.1 WK194 which, along with WK195, was hand-built at the Hursley Park experimental workshops. (Via Martyn Chorlton)

Swift F.2

Development

The next variant in the Swift family achieved the 'late in the day' remit for a fighter fitted with four Aden cannons rather than two. This, on the surface, straightforward modification of the original Swift F.1 design, created a host of unforeseen problems and jeopardised the future of the aircraft.

Design

The additional cannons were fitted into the lower forward fuselage as per the Swift F.1, but the extra ammunition needed had to be housed in the wing root. This resulted in an extension of the inboard leading edge, which looked an ideal solution on the drawing board but would cause serious geometric changes to the entire wing.

When the first Swift F.2, WK214, began flight testing in 1953, the new 'kinked' wing design quickly displayed its tendency to be completely unforgiving. The wing root extension completely changed the flow of air and when even the slightest g-force was applied above Mach 0.85, an uncontrollable pitch-up occurred. Despite the correct control input being implemented by the pilot, this did not stop the aircraft from flipping onto its back. As long as the aircraft was at altitude, a recovery could take place, but this was of little consolation to the pilot.

Modifications were applied in attempt to resolve the problem, including wing fences fitted to the top of the wing and the leading edges of the outer wings were extended to give a 'saw-tooth' profile. This was marginally effective but a cure was eventually found by moving the Centre of Gravity (CofG) further forward, which entailed loading a large amount of ballast into the nose. While this cured the back flip, the cost was a reduction in high-altitude performance.

Operational service

The Swift F.2 joined 56 Squadron on 30 August 1954, a unit that was still trying to find its feet with the Swift F.1. Like the earlier mark, 56 Squadron's association with the Swift F.2 was destined to be short and as just 17 were ever built, the aircraft only ever served briefly with the A&AEE and the RAE.

Production

Seventeen production aircraft to specification F105P were built under contract 6/Acft/5969/CB.5(b) (November 1950). Aircraft were WK199, WK214-WK221 and WK239-WK246. WK243 was retained by Supermarine for experimental work.

Technical data – Swift F.2	
ENGINE	One Rolls-Royce Avon RA.3/105
WINGSPAN	32.35ft
LENGTH	41ft ½in
HEIGHT	13ft ½in
WING AREA	306.2 sq ft
ARMAMENT	Four 30mm Aden cannon

Possibly one of the only air to air photographs of a Swift F.2 in service with 56 Squadron (and a poor one at that!). This is WK242, one of just six that served with the squadron from August 1954 to March 1955. (Via Martyn Chorlton)

Swift F.3

Development

The Swift F.3 was attempt to give Supermarine's waning fighter a little more power by introducing the Rolls-Royce Avon 114 engine with reheat. It was hoped this latest mark would help keep the RAF interested in the Swift, which by this time was not only causing negative stirrings on the line but also at the most senior of levels.

Design

On the surface, the F.3 was no different from the F.2, the only difference being the Avon 114 afterburning turbojet, which could produce 9,450lb of thrust when the throttle was pushed through the gate. The engine had already been trialled in a Swift F.1 but this appears not have revealed a major design fault. The problem was that the reheat could not be engaged above 20,000ft, which was another nail the Swift's coffin with regard to being accepted by the RAF as a high-altitude interceptor.

The Swift F.3 also featured fence's outboard of the 'kink' of each wing which went some way towards curing the pitch-up problems encountered by the F.2. Later, vortex generators were also fitted to the top and bottom of the tail surfaces which improved elevator control when flying at high Mach speeds.

Operational service

The Swift F.3 was destined to never enter RAF service and, of the 25 built, only the first off the production line, WK247, carried out any significant flying. WK247 did carry out an impressive display at the 1953 SBAC air show at Farnborough, demonstrating to full effect an energetic take-off using full reheat. The second aircraft, WK248, was the most extensively tested by the A&AEE at Boscombe Down.

The majority of the F.3s built did serve one practical purpose as ground instructional airframes after being delivered to the RAF by Supermarine and placed directly into storage.

Production

Twenty-five Swift F.3s were built to specification F105P under contract 6/Acft/5969/CB.5(b) (November 1950). Aircraft were WK247 to WK271.

Technical data – Swift F.3	
ENGINE	One 7,175lb (dry), 9,450lb (wet) Rolls-Royce Avon 114
WINGSPAN	32.35ft
LENGTH	41ft ½in
HEIGHT	13ft ½in
WING AREA	306.2 sq ft
ARMAMENT	Four 30mm Aden cannon

Swift F.3 WK248 during trials with the A&AEE at Boscombe Down. The aircraft was sold to the College of Aeronautics in 10 December 1956 for use as a ground instructional airframe. (Via Martyn Chorlton)

Swift F.4

Development

Despite only nine Swift F.4s ever being built, including the prototype, the mark finally brought hope that some of the fighter's handling problems had finally been cured. It was also the only variant that finally brought some positive achievement to the Swift by breaking the World Air Speed Record in 1953.

Design

The Swift F.4 was not a new build and the prototype, WK198, was the third production F.1, which was redesignated as the Type 546. It was modified with four Aden cannons, a 7,500lb Avon RA.7R with reheat, a saw-toothed wing and a variable-incidence tailplane. On the latter were pinned the hopes that the pitch-up characteristic of earlier marks could be removed.

Service

WK198, in its new guise as the F.4, was first flown by Mike Lithgow on 2 May 1953 and, after only nine test flights, it took part in the Coronation Flypast at Odiham on 15 July. On his return from Odiham, Lithgow suffered a compressor blade failure and was forced to make a power off landing at Chilbolton without further damage. Several engine failures followed, despite the same engine apparently causing no problem in the Hawker Hunter. It was later found that a different compressor blade was being used in the Swift's engine and once these were replaced no further problems occurred.

After taking part in the 1953 SBAC show, Lithgow flew WK198 to Tripoli for an attempt on the World's Absolute Air Speed Record, which at that time was in the hands of the USA and the F-86D. On 26 September 1953, Lithgow set a new record of 737.3mph which was, frustratingly, reduced to 735.7mph after a faulty speed camera's shutter was corrected. A follow up attempt produced an average of 743mph over two runs but, on the third, the reheat failed and the speed could not be ratified. Further attempts were about to be made when the news came through that a Douglas Skyray had raised the bar to 752.94mph on 3 October; a speed out of reach for the F.4.

One of the eight production F.4s, WK275, was fitted with an all-flying tailplane and datum trimmed and, after testing by A&AEE test pilots, was described as having superb handling. However, there was an important reheat problem, which meant that the aircraft would have to descend to 20,000ft to relight it, which brought about the premature end to the mark in favour of the low-level Swift FR.5. Further orders for 198 F.4s were cancelled and, of the eight production aircraft, four of them were converted to FR.5 standard.

Production

One prototype ex-F.1, WK198, was converted to F.4 and eight pre-production aircraft, WK272 to WK279, were delivered between November 1954 and June 1955. Four of these, WK274, WK276, WK277 and WK278, were all converted to FR.5.

The order later increased by 58 aircraft, WM583-WM596, WM621-WM656, WN124-WN127 and WV949-WV952. XD361 ordered as replacement but all cancelled on 20 March 1956.

XA957-XA993, XB102-XB151, XB169-XB185 and XB206-XB241 (140). Ordered under contract 6/Acft/8509 (April 1951) to have been built by Shorts. XA104-XF109 were also ordered, but the entire contract was cancelled.

Technical data – Swift F.4	
ENGINE	One 7,500lb Rolls-Royce Avon RA.7R
WINGSPAN	32.32ft
LENGTH	41.45ft
HEIGHT	13.2ft
WING AREA	320.7 sq ft
TARE WEIGHT	13,136lb
LOADED WEIGHT	19,764lb
MAX SPEED	709mph at sea level
RANGE	493 miles
RATE OF CLIMB	14,540 ft/min
CEILING	39,000ft
ARMAMENT	Four 30mm Aden cannon

Swift F.4 WK198 with Mike Lithgow at the controls during a test flight prior to leaving for North Africa for an attempt on the World Absolute Speed Record. (Via Martyn Chorlton)

Swift FR.5

Development

By now it was clear that the Swift was unsuitable for its intended role as a high-altitude interceptor. It was decided that the next mark would operate in the low-level high-speed tactical reconnaissance role which resulted in the Type 549 Swift FR.5. Intended as a replacement for the Meteor FR.9, the Swift FR.5 was by far the most successful and most produced example of the breed.

Design

The FR.5 was effectively an F.4 with a longer nose to accommodate a trio of F.95 cameras; one facing forward and two in opposing oblique positions. The camera installation was first trialled in a converted F.1 WK200. The only other difference was the armament, which reverted to a pair of 30mm Aden cannon as per the original F.1.

The first production aircraft was XD903 and this made its maiden flight on 27 May 1955 in the hands of Les Colquhoun. The next two, XD904 and XD905, were both fitted with clear-view canopies and a 220-gallon ventrally mounted drop tank, raising the Swift's total fuel capacity to 998 gallons.

Operational service

From February 1956, the Swift FR.5 began to equip 2 Squadron in place of the Meteor FR.9 at Geilenkirchen in West Germany. 79 Squadron at Wunstorf followed in June, both units operating as part of the Tactical Air Force under NATO control.

The FR.5 was a good performer in the reconnaissance role and, in May 1957, a pair of 79 Squadron Swifts came first in the second NATO Annual Reconnaissance Competition called 'Royal Flush'. The RAF jets were competing against a collection of Allied RF-84F Thunderjets in an exercise that required a visual reconnaissance with photographic confirmation of a target area 260 nautical miles long, captured below 500ft. The competition was won by an FR.5 again two years later.

A third unit, 4 Squadron, was reformed at Gütersloh with the FR.5 in December 1960, taking on the aircraft of 79 Squadron, which had disbanded at the same time. 2 and 4 Squadrons continued to operate the FR.5 until March 1961 when they both re-equipped with the Hunter FR.10.

Production

WK274, WK276-WK278, WK280-WK281, WK287-WK307 and WK309-WK315 (35) were all converted and diverted from the F.4 contract. WN314 was built as an FR.5.

XD903-XD930, XD948-XD988 and XE105-XE116 (113). Ordered under contract 6/Acft/9463 as 81 FR.5 and 32 PR.6, XE133-XE164. Only 58 FR.5s were built out of the whole order and the PR.6 never left the drawing board.

Technical data – Swift FR.5	
ENGINE	One 7,175lb (9,450lb with reheat) Rolls-Royce Avon RA.7R/114
WINGSPAN	32.33ft
LENGTH	42.26ft
HEIGHT	13.2ft
WING AREA	327.7 sq ft
TARE WEIGHT	13,435lb
LOADED WEIGHT	21,673lb
MAX SPEED	713mph at sea level
CLIMB	40,000ft in 4.69 min
RANGE	630 miles
RATE OF CLIMB	14,660 ft/min
CEILING	45,800ft
ARMAMENT	Two 30mm Aden cannon
CAMERAS	Three F.95 cameras; one facing forward and two mounted as opposing obliques

Three Swift FR.5s of the RAF Benson Ferry Unit in March 1956 prior to being delivered to 2 Squadron at Geilenkirchen in West Germany. XD908 and XD916 were both SOC on 27 June 1960 and XD914 on 30 May 1960. (*Aeroplane*)

Swift F.7

Development

As early as August 1952, Supermarine carried out a design study that featured a modified Swift carrying four Blue Sky (later renamed Skyflash) air-to-air missiles, four Aden guns and a radar guidance equipment. The design study would evolve into the Swift F.7, the final mark of this troubled series of aircraft.

Design

The proportions of the Swift F.7 were larger than its predecessors. To accommodate the continuous-wave radar, the nose was extended giving the fighter a length of 43.7ft and the wing span was increased to 36.08ft. Power was provided by an uprated Avon 116 engine with reheat while control was further improved over the FR.5 with a slab tailplane and datum trimming.

F.4 WK279 was used as a trials aircraft for the F.7, was modified to the same aerodynamic standard and was fitted with detachable launchers for the Blue Sky missiles. WK279 successfully launched three missiles in October 1955.

Operational service

The first of two prototype F.7s, XF774 made its maiden flight in early April 1956 followed by XF780 in June. The first production F.7, XF113, flew for the first time in August when all three aircraft plus WK279 were sent to Boscombe Down for handling trials and to establish limiting speed and Mach number. Fitted with pylons only, the maximum speed allowed was 600kts (Mach 0.92) up to 20,000ft, and with missiles fitted, this was reduced to 580kts. XF113 and XF774 spent most of their short career with the A&AEE and ETPS while XF780 was transferred to the MoS and was briefly designated as a PR.7, suggesting cameras may have been carried in the nose rather than a radar at some stage.

Production aircraft XF115 to XF124 were sent to Valley from December 1956, later serving with 1 GWDS (Guided Weapons Development Squadron) at Valley, which was formed on 1 June 1957. All of these aircraft were the first British fighters to be equipped with guided weapons.

By November 1958, the missile trials were over and the ten Swift F.7s on strength were scattered across the country on various trials including aquaplaning and braking tests at Waterbeach and Filton. By 2 February 1960, all ten were SOC.

Production

F.4 WK279 was modified to F.7 standard. XF774 and XF780 prototypes were ordered under contract 6/Acft/9929 (October 1953) as Blue Sky missile launchers.

XF113-XF129, XF155-XF180, XF196-XF217 and XF244-XF253 (75). Ordered under contract 6/Acft/9757 but only 12 (XF113-XF124) were built. XF249-XF253 were cancelled on 19 March 1954 while the rest were cancelled on 20 March 1956.

Technical data – Swift F.7	
ENGINE	One 7,550lb (dry) 9,950lb (reheat) Rolls-Royce Avon RA.7/116
WINGSPAN	36.08ft
LENGTH	43.7ft
HEIGHT	13.3ft
WING AREA	347.9 sq ft
TARE WEIGHT	13,735lb
LOADED WEIGHT	21,400lb
MAX SPEED	700mph at sea level
CLIMB	40,000ft in 16.75 min without reheat
RANGE	864 miles
CEILING	41,600ft

The prototype Swift F.7, XF774, which first flew in March 1956 only to serve with the A&AEE and the ETPS. The aircraft was transferred to RAE Farnborough as a structural test specimen on 10 June 1958, and we can only presume it was tested to destruction as it was SOC on 19 August. (Via Martyn Chorlton)

Scimitar

Development

The progressive development that saw the Type 508, 525 and 529 being produced finally bore fruit with the arrival of the Type 444, originally known as the N.113D, which would become the Scimitar F.1. It was destined to be the last aircraft solely designed and built by Supermarine and was certainly its most technologically challenging and innovative product to date.

Design

Compared to the development aircraft, the Scimitar had a longer nose and dorsal spine and was an area-rule design. Powered by a pair of 10,000lb Avon engines, the big fighter had all-swept flight services, flaps with boundary layer control, full length leading edge flaps and an all-moving anhedral tailplane. The aircraft was generally constructed of aluminium and chemical etching was used for the first time for precision components, of which there were many. Each wing was incredibly strong, being made up of three steel and an element of titanium was used in the spars. This was the first time titanium had been used in a British aircraft.

The wings had a 45° sweep and chord to thickness ratio of 8% which, despite the power available, was the reason why the Scimitar could never break the sound barrier. The wings could be hydraulically folded mid-span and an airbrake on each side of the rear fuselage was also hydraulically actuated. The 'artificial feel' flight controls were hydraulically powered as well and the pilot had the luxury of a pressurised climate-controlled cockpit and a Martin-Baker Mk 4C ejection seat.

Operational service

The first Type 544 Scimitar prototype, WT854, was flown by Mike Lithgow from Boscombe Down on 19 January 1956. Deck landing trials aboard HMS *Ark Royal* followed in April and by the end of the year the next two prototypes, WT859 and WW134, were also airborne. Early handling problems with the prototypes were quickly rectified with a dog-tooth and a fence fitted to each wing and the tail assembly was modified.

The Scimitar F.1 entered FAA service with 700X Flight IFTU (Intensive Flying Trials Unit) based at Ford. Operational service began with 803 Squadron at Lossiemouth in June 1958 followed by a tour of duty on HMS *Victorious* in September. Other operational units who flew the Scimitar were 736, 764, 764B, 800, 800B, 804 and 807 Squadrons. Second line units were RNAS Hal Far, AHU Lossiemouth, RNAY Fleetlands, NASU Brawdy, Airwork FRU, AAEE, RNAS Arbroath, RAE Bedford, RAE Farnborough and AHU Tengah/Sembawang. As well as HMS *Victorious*, the Scimitar was also operated from the following Royal Navy aircraft carriers; HMS *Ark Royal*, *Centaur*, *Eagle* and *Hermes*.

Intended for the air combat role, the Scimitar's high-altitude performance was not good and the Sea Vixen quickly claimed the role for itself. However, the Scimitar found itself, like the Swift, being more successful at low-levels as a strike fighter specialising in 'toss bombing' the Red Beard nuclear bomb. Those Scimitars designated to carry Red Beard were fitted with a Low Altitude Bombing System (LABS), which incorporated a toss bombing computer and a Blue Silk Doppler navigation radar.

Towards the end of its career and as its replacement the Buccaneer entered service, the Scimitar found itself serving in another unintended role. The Buccaneer S.1 was seriously underpowered and the only way it could take off from a carrier was with a low fuel load. Once airborne, the Buccaneer rendezvoused with a Scimitar tanker, filled up and then carried out a normal operation.

Production

Three production prototypes, WT854, WT859 and WW134, were ordered to specification N.113D and built as Type 544.

Main production order for 100 Scimitars (XD212-XD357) was under contract 6/Air/8812/CB.5(a) to specification N.113P.1, Naval Staff requirement NRA.17 as Type 544. Seventy-six aircraft built in the serial range D212 to XD357.

Technical data – Type 544 Scimitar F.1	
ENGINE	Two 10,000lb st Rolls-Royce Avon RA.24 or RA.28 and later 200 series
WINGSPAN	37ft 2in
WINGSPAN (folded)	20ft 6½in
LENGTH	55ft 3in
HEIGHT	17ft 4in
WING AREA	484.9 sq ft
SWEEPBACK	45° at 25% chord
EMPTY WEIGHT	23,962lb
LOADED WEIGHT	34,200lb
MAX SPEED	640 kt (Mach 0.968) at sea level. 587 kt at 30,000ft
CLIMB	45,000ft in 6.65 min
RANGE	1,422 miles at 35,000ft
CEILING	46,000ft
ARMAMENT	Four 30mm Aden cannon and four 1,000lb bombs or four Bullpup air-to-ground missiles, or four Sidewinder air-to-air missiles. Alternatively, four 200-gal drop tanks

Above left: The first production Scimitar F.1, XD212, which first flew on 11 January 1957. Following trials and development work with Supermarine, the aircraft was delivered to the FAA on 4 June 1958. It was lost on 20 September 1961 whilst serving with 736 Squadron at Lossiemouth after it spun in at Raich Hill, Forgie, eight miles northwest of Huntley. The pilot did not eject. (*Aeroplane*)

Above right: The prototype Scimitar F.1, WT854, pictured during initial deck landing trials aboard HMS *Ark Royal* in April 1956. The big fighter served on until November 1964 and by 1967 had ended its days as hulk at P&EE Foulness. (*Aeroplane*)

The Drawing Board

A compilation of the most significant projects which either reached the mock-up stage or never left the drawing board

A.D. Submarine Patrol Seaplane

Following the poor performance of the A.D. Navyplane, an improved version was designed called the A.D. Submarine Patrol Seaplane. It was intended as a replacement for the excellent Short Type 184, despite the fact that the aircraft was already adequately performing well in its intended role.

The specification was for a pusher biplane, powered by a 200hp Sunbeam engine and flown by a crew of two. The aircraft would be capable of carrying a Type 52A wireless, signal gear, marker buoys and carrier pigeon as well as four 100lb bombs. Contracts were placed for six aircraft, two to be built by Shorts, two by Phoenix and two by Supermarine. The latter was cancelled on 17 February 1917 because of the need for the N.1B Baby, while the

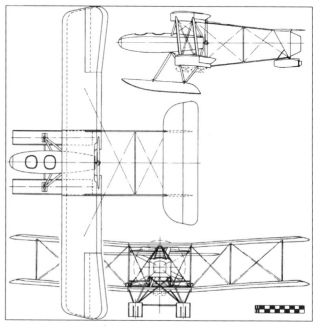

The A.D. Submarine Patrol Seaplane.

other manufacturer were asked to prepare detailed drawings. Working drawings had already been prepared by Supermarine but in the end the aircraft never materialised.

Submarine Patrol Seaplane Production
N24-N25 (2) ordered but CNX 17 February 1917 when design was nearing completion. Contracts were also issued to Shorts (N20-N21) and Phoenix (N22-N23) but all CNX

Technical data – A.D. Submarine Patrol Seaplane	
ENGINE	One 200hp Sunbeam
MAX SPEED	60kt
MINIMUM SPEED	35kt
CLIMB	6,000ft in less than 30 min
ARMAMENT	Four 100lb bombs

Transatlantic flying boat

A very ambitious design for a Transatlantic transport flying boat capable of carrying up to 24 passengers. Size is difficult to gauge but the wing span alone could not have been far short of 100ft.

Technical data – Transatlantic flying boat	
ENGINE	Three Bristol Jupiter or three Napier Lion

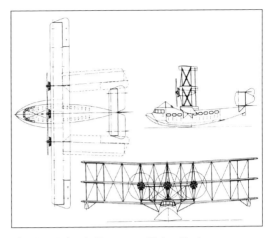

The Transatlantic Passenger Flying-Boat.

Shark flying boat

The Shark was a triplane flying boat capable of carrying a torpedo under each wing, at which point the assembly could be folded back along the line of the fuselage. The aggressive design also incorporated five gun positions, two forward of the wings, two more behind and a fifth in front of the tail assembly.

Technical data – Shark Triplane flying boat	
ENGINE	Two Napier Lion
WEIGHT	14,000lb
ARMAMENT	Up to five gun positions and two torpedoes

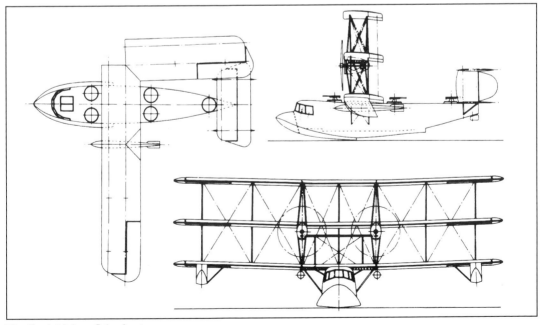

The Shark triplane flying boat.

Fighter flying boat

In 1921, the Air Ministry issued a list of basic requirements for a D or R Type 6 single-seat flying boat that could operate from a ship or in an amphibian guise. The requirement later went to the Fairey Flycatcher, which was not a flying boat but a conventional land-plane.

Supermarine settled on the Sea King to meet the requirement but, in the background, a second design, unlike anything ever seen before, was for a tractor amphibian powered by an air-cooled Jupiter or Jaguar engine. The design was clearly way ahead of its time and without doubt exhibited the basic layout of the Walrus and the Sea Otter, which were still another 12 years away.

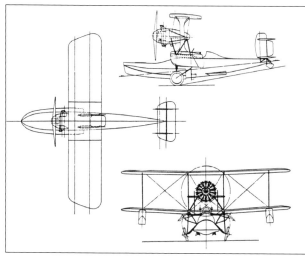

The Type 6 single-seat fighter flying boat.

Technical data – Single-seat fighter flying boat	
ENGINE	One Armstrong Siddeley Jupiter or Jaguar air-cooled radial
WINGSPAN	29ft
LENGTH	24ft
MAX SPEED	120kt at 10,000ft

Scylla

Development

When the First World War came to an end, the Air Ministry began tendering for designs of an aircraft that was worthy of replacing the successful Porte-Felixstowe F series of flying boats. Supermarine began work, in 1919, on a twin-engined design referred to as the Shark torpedo carrier. By 1921, R J Mitchell had produced a design with Rolls-Royce engines which could operate in both military and civilian forms.

A contract to build a five-seat military boat/seaplane, called the Scylla was received in 1921.

Design

The Scylla began as a monoplane, powered by a pair of Rolls-Royce Eagle IX engines that were mounted on pylons above the wing. A 35hp Green auxiliary engine was also fitted inside the hull to drive a water propeller for taxying. The cockpit was positioned just forward of the mainplane in a rather clumsy looking raised section while only one air gunner position was provided in the nose.

By March 1923, work on the Scylla began to lose momentum as the company began to focus on the Swan instead. However, construction of the Scylla continued and, serialled N174, the flying boat was prepared for taxying trials in February 1924.

A second Scylla design, showing a triplane configuration, never materialised. Power was planned to be a pair of 550hp Rolls-Royce Condor engines and the pilot's cockpit was extended rearwards, providing a second cockpit and a second air gunner's position.

The hull of the sole Scylla, N174, outside Supermarine's head office in Hazel Road, Woolston. The aircraft was about to leave for the M&AEE at Felixstowe for taxying trials. (*Aeroplane*)

Service
Very little is known about the fate of the Scylla, other than that it was delivered to Air Ministry and onwards to Felixstowe for taxying trials. It was never flown and was most likely scrapped at Felixstowe not long after.

Production
One aircraft, N174, ordered under contract 248426/21 as a five-seat military seaplane.

Technical data – Scylla	
ENGINE	(Monoplane) Two Rolls-Royce Eagle IX. (Triplane) Two 550hp Rolls-Royce Condor

Sea Urchin early
A single aircraft, designed by Frank Holroyd and R J Mitchell, was ordered by the Air Ministry but construction did not begin owing to technical difficulties.

Technical data – Sea Urchin	
ENGINE	One 600hp Rolls-Royce Condor V-12
WINGSPAN	24ft (under)
MAX SPEED	200mph (estimated)

S.4 (Schneider) High-Performance

A proposal for a high-speed development version of the S.4, which in turn led to the S.5

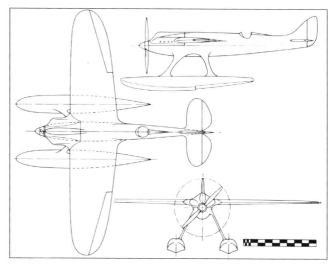

Right: **The S.4 high-speed development variant.**

S.5 (Schneider) Strut-braced

A Joseph Smith design to strut-brace the Supermarine S.5 but inevitably wire-bracing was used.

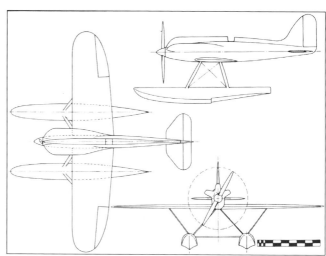

Right: **Proposed S.5 with strut-bracing.**

S.6 (Schneider) Biplane

In an effort to lower the alighting speed of the S.6 to a more manageable 90mph, one proposal was to turn the S.6 into a biplane. With little modification, an upper wing could be added, more than doubling the wing area and, in theory, lowering the landing speed.

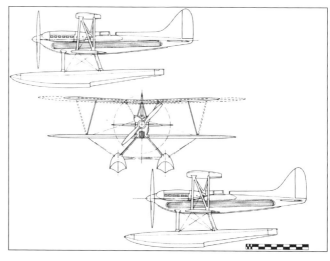

Right: **One solution to lowering the alighting speed of the S.6 was to fit a second upper wing.**

Type 179 'Giant'

It was Oswald Short and his efforts to produce a better design than the Dornier Do X that brought about military Specification R.6/28. Even though it was a Short Brother's design which prompted the specification, it was customary to circulate it to other aircraft manufacturers, including Supermarine which received a 'request for tender' on 17 November 1928.

Supermarine's design entry for the specification was, unsurprisingly, beaten by the Short Sarafand, but a separate request, 20/28, received on 18 May 1929 called for a civilian variant capable of carrying 40 passengers.

The R.6/29 Type 179 was an all-metal high-wing monoplane powered by six inline engines in three nacelles driving both tractor and pusher propellers. The engines were mounted on pylons above the

Right: Artist's impression of the Type 179 with Bristol Jupiter engines.

Below: Another artist's impression, this time with Rolls-Royce Buzzard engines.

wing and, below it, large sponsons were attached which would have given the flying boat the handling of a trimaran. Passengers would have not only been accommodated with the fuselage but also inside the leading edge of the very thick Raf 34 aerofoil.

By 1930, the design had changed to a more traditional outer wing float design and the engines had now increased to eight in a four nacelle layout. By now, the passengers were entirely seated in the fuselage. Work began in April 1931, under contract 13135/30, and the aircraft was registered as G-ABLE and called the 'Giant'. Work continued into early 1932 and even during the construction, the design of the engine nacelles and tail surfaces were changed.

Unfortunately, on 19 January 1932, the government cancelled the contract due to economic constraints and, despite reaching an advanced stage, the Type 179 'Giant' was scrapped.

Technical data – Type 179	
ENGINE	Six 850/900hp Rolls-Royce H (later eight 1,030hp Rolls-Royce Buzzard MS from December 1931)
WINGSPAN	185ft
LENGTH	104ft 6in
HEIGHT	32ft
WING AREA	4,720 sq ft
EMPTY WEIGHT	49,390lb
LOADED WEIGHT	75,090lb
FUEL CAPACITY	2,175 gal
MAX SPEED	145mph at sea level
ALIGHTING SPEED	72.5mph
RANGE	700 miles (normal) or 1,300 miles with a lower fuel load and a speed of 108.5mph
MAX RATE OF CLIMB	750 ft/min at sea level
SERVICE CEILING	11,000ft
ENDURANCE	12hrs

Type 316-318 B.12/36 Bomber

It was in 1936 that the Air Ministry issued Specification B.12/36 for the first four-engined heavy bomber for the RAF. Armstrong Whitworth, Shorts and Supermarine all tendered for this huge project.

Supermarine came up with the Type 316, a bomber that could carry its weapon load in the wings and the fuselage in a similar, scaled-up version of the Whitley. Various power plants were explored, including the fledgling Rolls-Royce Merlin, the Bristol Hercules and the Napier Dagger.

Top speed was, optimistically, estimated at between 325 and 360mph, a cruising speed of around 260mph, a ceiling of 30,000ft and an impressive range of up to 3,000 miles.

Despite being low down on the Air Ministry's preferred design list, the Type 316 was actually selected with the Hercules engines. However, so many changes were suggested and implemented by both the Air Ministry and Supermarine that the design was redesignated the Type 317 and two prototypes, L6889 and L6890, were ordered on 22 March 1937.

Above: The Type 179, pictured at an advanced stage of construction on the day it was cancelled on 19 January 1932.

Right: The Type 317 built to Specification B.12/36, which was eventually fulfilled by the Short Stirling.

Below: What the Type 317 would have looked like if completed.

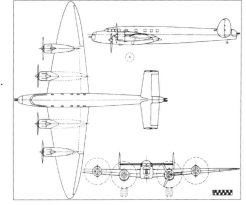

The Type 317, as it appeared, virtually complete, before the Luftwaffe destroyed it in an air raid in September 1940.

When R J Mitchell died, the Air Ministry wisely decided, with the benefit of hindsight, to order the Short S.29 Stirling as a back-up following the change at Supermarine's design helm.

Supermarine continued to worked on the project, producing drawings of the Type 318 with Merlin engines, although work on this project came to a halt in July 1937.

Whilst one prototype was nearing completion and the second was laid down, the Luftwaffe bombed the Woolston works on 26 September 1940, destroying the Type 317. By November, the Air Ministry had cancelled the order and the S.29 Stirling became the RAF's first four-engine bomber.

Type 312

The last aircraft design before R J Mitchell's death in June 1937, the Type 312 was basically a Spitfire Mk I fitted with four 20mm Oerlikon cannons fitted into a modified wing. Both the radiator and oil cooler were transferred from under the wing to a duct below the fuselage in a similar layout that would later be adopted by the North American Mustang.

Type 305

While retaining the elegant lines of the Spitfire's mainplane and tail surfaces, the Type 305 was Supermarine's entry for Specification F.9/35, calling for a two-seat four-gun turret fighter to replace the Hawker Demon.

The Type 305's fuselage was virtually a new build to provide room for the gunner and his remote control four gun turret, designed for four .303in Browning machine guns, which was later changed to .303in Lewis machine guns. The cooling system was also changed, with a large air intake under the nose, with a radiator housed inside. The two-seat fighter was also fitted with dive brakes in the wings but no forward firing guns.

The specification was won, head and shoulders above the rest by the Boulton Paul Defiant and, to a lesser extent by the Hawker Hotspur. The Bristol 147 and the Type 305 fell by the wayside.

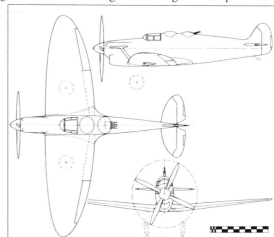

The one and only attempt to turn the Spitfire into a two-seat four-gun turret fighter.

Technical data – Type 305	
ENGINE	One Rolls-Royce Merlin
WINGSPAN	37ft
LENGTH	30ft 6in
LOADED WEIGHT	5,650lb
MAX SPEED	315mph at 15,000ft

Type 324, 325 and 327

The elegantly designed Type 324 and 325 came about in response to the Air Ministry issuing Specification F.18/37. The specification called for a heavily armed interceptor armed with 12 .303in machine guns and the ability to reach at least 400mph. F.18/37 was a hotly contested specification and, as well as the two Supermarine entries, the Bristol F.18/37, Gloster F.18/37, Hawker Tornado and Typhoon were also vying for the order. The winner was the Typhoon, which eventually entered service in 1941.

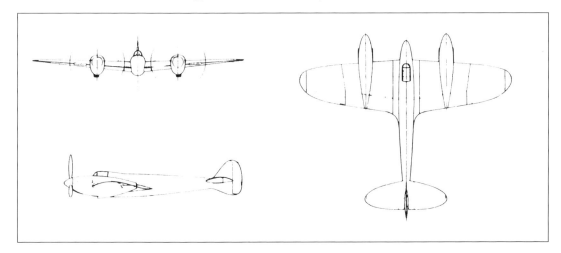

Above: The Type 327, designed to Specification F.18/37.

Right: The Type 327, twin-engined six-cannon fighter mock-up pictured in 1936.

The Type 324 was powered by a pair of Merlins in a traditional tractor layout while the Type 327 was a pusher arrangement; both had a tricycle undercarriage. Both shared the elliptical mainplane design of the Spitfire and the twelve .303in machine guns were positioned in groups of six in the outer wing. The design was revisited in August 1938, resulting in the Type 327, once again powered by two Merlins but with fitted with six 20mm cannons, buried at the wing roots, very close to the fuselage, for concentrated fire. The Type 327 did reach the mock-up stage but by now priorities had moved and World War Two was just around the corner.

Technical data – Type 327	
ENGINE	Two Rolls-Royce Merlin
WINGSPAN	40ft
LENGTH	33ft 6in
LOADED WEIGHT	11,312lb
MAX SPEED	465mph at 22,000ft

Type 391 'High Performance Fighter'

During the design and development stages of the Spiteful in 1943, Supermarine took the opportunity to dispatch a brochure to the Air Ministry titled, 'High-Performance Aeroplane for the Royal Navy'. This was the Type 391, which was designed to operate as a fighter from aircraft carriers and have the dual ability to act as a strike aircraft able to carry an 18in Mk XV aerial torpedo. It also had a fixed armament of 20mm Hispano Mk V cannons and bombs or RPs.

The fighter used the Spiteful/Seafang wing and the sturdy undercarriage was mounted into a wide centre-section that also housed leading edge air intakes and coolant radiators. Power was to be provided by the 3,550hp Rolls-Royce 'Eagle' engine driving large four-bladed, contra-rotating propellers.

Technical data – Type 391	
ENGINE	One 3,550hp, Rolls-Royce 46-H-24 'Eagle' 24 cylinder
WINGSPAN	43ft 6in
LENGTH	39ft 9in
WING AREA	335 sq. ft.
MAX WEIGHT (fighter)	15,750lb
MAX WEIGHT (torpedo-bomber)	17,250lb
MAX SPEED	546mph at 25,000ft
ARMAMENT	Four 20mm cannon Hispano Vs. Bombs, rockets or one 18in Mk XV aerial torpedo

Spitfire F.23

The Spitfire F.23 was, effectively, the F.22 with a new wing that was designed with a greater incidence, raising the leading edge by 2in. The modification was designed to give the pilot a better view over the nose during flight, increase the top speed and improve the dive performance.

The new wing, which was hand-built, was attached to Mk VIII JG204 and flight tested in July 1944. Results were disappointing and a completely new prototype, making use of F.21, PP139, was redesignated the F.23 and named 'Valiant'. Once again, though, performance and general handling were not good and the F.23 was shelved.

Type 524

Designed to Specification R.2/48 (OR.213) for a large reconnaissance seaplane, the Type 524 was Supermarine's last maritime design. The giant aircraft was to have a span of 148ft and was optimistically powered by just four Bristol Proteus propeller-turbines. Designs were also put forward for the Blackburn B-78, the Saunders-Roe P.104 and P.162 and a development of the Short Shetland, the PD.2. The specification was later modified in the early 1950s to R.112D but, by then, post-war thinking was no longer in tune with the operation of large flying boats.

Technical data – Type 524	
ENGINE	Four Bristol Proteus
WINGSPAN	148ft
LOADED WEIGHT	117,110lb
MAX SPEED	338kt at 24,000ft

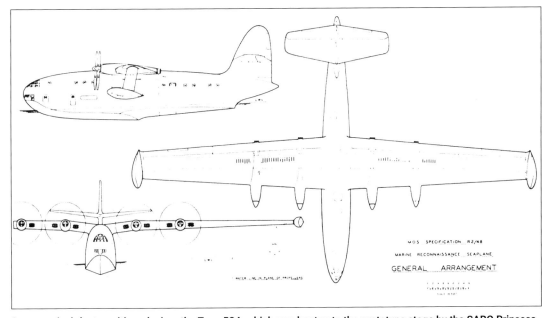

Supermarine's last maritime design, the Type 524, which was beaten to the prototype stage by the SARO Princess.

Type 521

Designed to Air Ministry Specification E.6/48, the Handley Page HP.88 was a research aircraft designed to test the aerodynamics of the Victor bomber.

Effectively a scaled down version of the Victor, the aircraft was originally designed by General Aircraft (GAL) but this work was moved to Brough when GAL merged with Blackburn.

The Handley Page HP.88, VX330, whose fuselage was designated the Type 521 and built by Supermarine. (Via Martyn Chorlton)

Supermarine's role in this aircraft was a major one, as they were contracted to build the fuselage, which was based on the Type 510. Supermarine gave the fuselage the designation Type 521 and delivered it to Brough in early 1951. HP.88 VX330 was first flown from Carnaby on 21 June 1951 but after flight testing, the aircraft suffered from pitching problems at high speeds. After delivery to Handley Page, the aircraft was transferred to Stansted on 6 August 1951 for more tests.

On 26 August 1951, and with just 14 hours on the airframe, the HP.88 carried out a high-speed pass over Stansted in preparation for that year's SBAC. Unfortunately, the aircraft broke up mid-air, killing the pilot before any useful data was recorded.

Type 545

The Type 545 was designed in response to Air Ministry Specification F.105D2 for a new naval fighter. The aircraft was designed to operate above Mach 1 and its crescent shaped wing reflected this. The single Avon turbojet was fed air via a nose air intake which had a central, bullet-shaped centrebody and this was employed in the English Electric P.1 and later the Lightning.

Two aircraft were ordered, under contract 6/Acft/7771, in February 1952. The first, XA181, was constructed and completed at Hursley Park. The second aircraft, XA186, was cancelled before construction began on 8 October 1954 and the entire project was also dissolved on 23 March 1956.

XA181 remained in store until the mid-1950s when it was donated to the College of Aeronautics at Cranfield. After several year's use as an instructional airframe, the only completed Type 545 was scrapped in 1967.

Technical data – Type 545	
POWERPLANT	One 9,500lb (dry), 14,500lb (reheat) Rolls-Royce Avon RA.14R or RA.35R or RB.106
SPAN	39ft
LENGTH	47ft
MAX WEIGHT	20,147lb
MAX SPEED	(RA.14R) 858mph at 36,000ft
MAX SPEED	(RA.14R) Mach 1.3. (RA.35R & RB.106) Mach 1.68
SERVICE CEILING	53,000ft
ARMAMENT	Four 30mm ADEN cannons

The sole Type 545, XA181, residing at the College of Aeronautics at Cranfield after the project was cancelled in 1956. (Via Martyn Chorlton)

Type 553

The Type 553 or ER.134T Experimental Aircraft was a proposal for a research aircraft that was capable of reaching Mach 2.4 at 36,000ft. Power was to be provided by a single Rolls-Royce RB.106.

The Type 553 resembled the Douglas D-558- Skystreak but never rose beyond the proposal stage.

Swift PR.6

The Type 550 Swift PR.6 was to be an unarmed version of the Swift FR.5, designed to replace the in service Meteor PR.10.A single prototype, XF778, was ordered under contract 6/Acft/9929 in November 1952 but was cancelled on 25 April 1955.

Type 556

A single Type 556, XH451, was ordered as a 'Developed Scimitar' to specification NA/38 from Vickers Ltd under contract 6/Air/11268/CB.5(b) on 23 September 1954. The aircraft was a two-seat FAW version of the Scimitar with a Ferranti Air Pass radar and guided weapons. A mock-up was built but this was suspended on 27 April 1955 and cancelled on 25 July 1955.

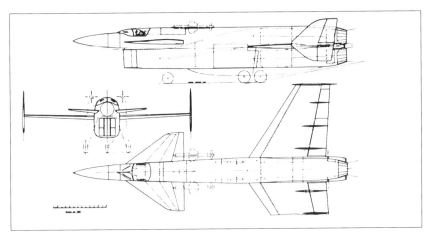

The Type 559.

Type 559

On 15 January 1955, Specification F.155T was issued with the Air Ministry's latest requirements for a two-seat, radar-equipped fighter capable of carrying four missiles. The detailed performance demands included the requirement to intercept and destroy targets flying at up to Mach 2 at 60,000ft. Once Mach 2.3 was reached at 60,000ft, a rocket booster would kick in and, after running for 45 seconds, pushed the aircraft to 92,000ft in a similar way to the Me163.

The Type 559 displayed a host of novel design features, including a canard configuration that promised a far superior lift coefficient than the traditional layout. The foreplane was all-moving and its tips were cropped to dissipate the buffet normally experienced with a delta shape. Any vortices that could be created by the canard, especially at high-angles of attack, were dealt with by large end plates on each wingtip. Each wing had an integral fuel tank capable of carrying 960 gallons.

This complex aircraft was designed to be developed in stages, including the fully-automatic control and guidance systems which would evolve with the Type 559. Operational equipment could have allowed the Type 559 to carry out programmed climbs, instrument landings, manoeuvre holding and pre-selection heading, heights and speeds. Even more advanced capabilities such as air interception control and automatic navigation would be added during the development program.

Despite being the favourite to win the F.155T specification competition, all contestants suffered at the hands of the infamous 1957 Defence White Paper, which abolished all work on manned fighters in favour of ground-controlled missiles. However, there was one requirement still going begging and that was the need for a low-level bomber in the tactical strike and reconnaissance (TSR) role to replace the Canberra.

Technical data – Type 559	
ENGINE	Two 27,000lb (with reheat) de Havilland PS.26/1 and two 5,000lb de Havilland Spectre Junior rocket motors
WINGSPAN	42ft
LENGTH	68ft 3in
HEIGHT	15ft 3in
WING AREA	615 sq ft
FOREPLANE AREA	202 sq ft
SWEEPBACK	27.5°
EMPTY WEIGHT	41,485lb
LOADED WEIGHT	62,190lb
MAX SPEED	Mach 2.5
RADIUS OF ACTION	150 miles
DURATION	32min
ARMAMENT	Four DH Blue Jay (Firestreak) or Vickers Red Hebe (development of Red Dean)

Type 571

General Operational Requirement (GOR) 339 encompassed the need for an aircraft that could operate at low-level with tactical strike weapons and carry out medium-altitude bombing. The aircraft should also be able to operate in all-weather conditions and still carry out reconnaissance and photographic

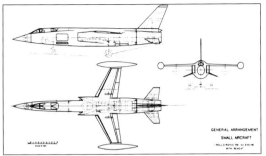 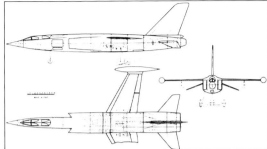

Above left: **The 40,000lb Type 571.**

Above right: **The 81,000lb Type 571.**

roles including limited night coverage. What emerged was the TSR.2, a joint project between Vickers-Armstrongs and English Electric, which would later merge into BAC.

Two project designs were submitted by Supermarine for GOR 339, both called the Type 571, but one weighed in at 40,000lb (Small) and the other at 81,000lb (Large). The smaller Type 571 was powered by a single RB.142 and the larger with two, both with reheat. Both would be equipped with low-level terrain capability and a host of sophisticated electronic equipment. The latter included an inertial guidance navigation system, sideways and forwards-looking radar, Doppler with an unrolling map and an automatic bomb delivery capability.

The 80,000lb Type 571 was actually chosen to be married with the English Electric proposal to become the TSR.2, although Supermarine would have preferred the smaller version. The smaller Type 571 could have seamlessly followed the Scimitar production line at South Marston as the next generation of naval fighters. However, it was not to be and the TSR.2 took a different direction, which did not have a happy ending for BAC or the British aviation industry as a whole.

Technical data – Type 571 (TSR.2 Two)	
ENGINE	(Large) Two or One (Small) 14,000lb (22,700lb with reheat) Rolls Royce RB.142
WINGSPAN (Large)	41ft 6in
WINGSPAN (Small)	28ft
LENGTH (Large)	77ft
LENGTH (Small)	58ft
WING AREA (Large)	430 sq ft
WING AREA (Small)	200 sq ft
LOADED WEIGHT (Large)	81,225lb (internal fuel tanks full)
LOADED WEIGHT (Small)	40,220lb (internal fuel tanks full)
MAX SPEED	Mach 1.1 at sea level and Mach 2.3 at 36,000ft
INTERNAL FUEL (Large)	4,675 gal
INTERNAL FUEL (Small)	1,948 gal

Type 573 SST

In support of the Concorde development programme, Supermarine produced a design for a quarter-scale piloted model to Specification ER.197D, calling for a low-speed research aircraft. Type 573 was a slender-winged design that eventually led to the Handley Page HP.115, which successfully served as a low-speed trials aircraft from 1961 to 1974.

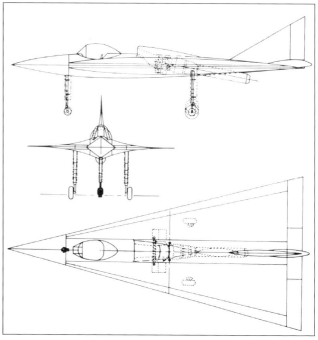

Right: The quarter-scale Type 573, which led to the creation of the Handley Page HP.115.

Type 576 Supersonic Scimitar

Although the original Scimitar could break the sound barrier in a shallow dive, it certainly could not manage it in level flight. Supermarine's solution was simply to give the Scimitar more power with uprated Avon engines and the added thrust of a pair of DH Spectre rocket boosters.

Presented in single or twin-seat arrangement, the Supersonic Scimitar had the potential to become a replacement for the Sea Vixen although, this in the end went to the Buccaneer.

Technical data – Type 576 Supersonic Scimitar	
ENGINE	Two Rolls-Royce Avon 300 Series and two de Havilland Spectre rocket boosters
WINGSPAN	41ft
LENGTH	61ft
LOADED WEIGHT	51,357lb
MAX SPEED	Mach 1.8 at 65,000ft

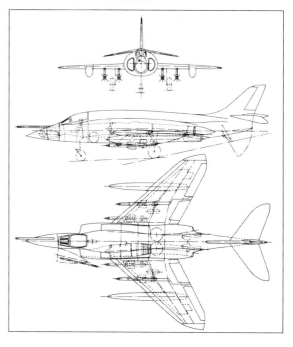

Right: The supersonic mixed-power Scimitar interceptor.

Supermarine Type Designations

Pemberton Billing

P.B. Glider (P.B.0)
P.B. Monoplane (P.B.1, 3 & 5)
P.B.1 (P.B.7)
P.B.1 ((Mod (P.B.9))
P.B.2 (P.B.11)
P.B.3
P.B.5 (P.B.21)
P.B.7 (P.B.19)
P.B.9 (P.B.13)
P.B.13 (P.B.17)
P.B.23E
P.B.25
P.B.27
P.B.29E NightHawk
P.B.31
P.B.31E NightHawk

Supermarine aircraft without type designations – 1916 to 1930

A.D. Boat
A.D Navyplane
N.1B Baby
Patrol Floatplane
Channel I & II
Sea King I & II
Sea Lion I, II & III
Sea Urchin
S.4
S.5
S.6
S.6B
Commercial Amphibian
Sea Eagle
Seal I & II
Swan
Scylla
Seagull I, II & III
Sparrow I & II
Sheldrake
Scarab
Seamew
Air Yacht
Southampton I
Solent/Nanok

Supermarine aircraft using Vickers sequence type designation – 1929 to 1960

178	Misc. Drawings
179	Monoplane flying boat
180	Civil
181	G.P. Amphibian
182 & 183	G.P. high and low-wing monoplane
184, 190, 233 & 234	Southampton II
185 & 188	Southampton X
186 & 187	S.6B 1931 mods
189	Southampton I
221, 226, 229 & 235	Southampton IV/ Scapa
222 & 301	Vildebeest floats
223, 228 & 307	Seagull V
224	F.7/30
225	Seagull type
227, 230 & 239	Southampton V/ Stranraer
231	Bomber transport
232 & 239	Monoplane flying boat
236, 315, 320 & 507	Walrus I & II
238	Biplane flying boat
240	Coastal landplane
300, 335, 336, 338, 341, 342, 343, 344, 345, 346 & 354	Spitfire prototype and I
302	Flying boat

303	Scapa development	366	Spitfire XII
304	Stranraer R.24/31 development	367	Spitfire PR.XIII
		369, 373 & 379	Spitfire XIV
305	F.9/35	371, 382 & 393	Spiteful
306	Atlantic mail boat	377 & 386	Seafire XV
308 & 310	High-performance flying boat	381	Seagull S.12/40
		382 & 396	Seafang
309, 326, 399 & 503	Sea Otter/Walrus development	384	Seafire XVII
		388	Seafire F.45 & F.47
311	F.7/34	389 & 390	Spitfire XIX
312 & 313	F.7/35 Spitfire	391	High performance fighter
314	R.1/36		
316, 317 & 318	B.12/36	392, 397, 398, 500, 513, 515, 538 & 542	Attacker E.10/44, F.1 & FB.2
319	Two-seat fighter		
321	Supermarine Mk IV gun turret	394	Spitfire F & PR.XVIII
322 & 380	S.24/37 'Dumbo'	395	Seafire XVIII
323	High-speed Spitfire	501	Spitfire export
324 & 325	F.18/37	502	Spitfire T.8
327	Cannon fighter	504	S.14/44 ASR
328	R.3/38 flying boat	505	Naval jet fighter N.9/47
329	Spitfire II	508, 522, 525, 529, 537, 539 & 555	
330 & 348	Spitfire III		
331 & 352	Spitfire VB	509	Spitfire T.9
332	Spitfire FN wing gun installation	510 & 514	E.10/44 Mod
		517, 520, 528, 531, 535, 541, 545, 546 & 551	Swift, F.1 to F.4
333	N.9/39 two-seat fighter		
334	S.6/39	521	HP.88 fuselage
337	Spitfire IV	523 & 526	F.3/48
339	NAD 925/39	524	R.2/48
347	S.12/40	530	Seagull ASR.I
349	Spitfire VC	532	E.41/46 developed
350	Spitfire VI	533	34mm Vickers cannon
351	Spitfire VII		
353	Spitfire PR.IV	543	Fighter
355	Spitfire V special	544, 556, 560, 562, 564, 565, 566, 567, 572 & 574	Scimitar F.1 Development, Naval & RAF
356	Spitfire F.21, 22 & 24		
357 & 375	Seafire IIC		
358 & 506	Seafire III	547a & b	Swift two-seat F.1 & F.4
359, 360, 368, 372 & 376	Spitfire VIII		
360	Spitfire VIID	548	Swift Naval F.4
361, 378 & 385	Spitfire IX/XVI	549	Swift FR.5
362 & 387	Spitfire PR.X	550	Swift PR.6
363 & 364	Spitfire tropical	552	Swift F.7
365, 370 & 374	Spitfire PR.XI	553	ER13T Experimental Research

554	OR.318
558	N113 prototype
559	Canard to GOR.339/ F155T
563	Scimitar Swiss Air Force
569	Guided powered bomb
571	Various projects to GOR.339
573	Quarter-Scale SST
576	Supersonic Scimitar

Glossary

A&AEE	Aeroplane & Armament Experimental Establishment
AFDU	Air Fighting Development Unit
AGS	Air Gunnery School
AHU	Aircraft Holding Unit
AMDP	Air Member for Development and Production
AST	Air Service Training Ltd
ATA	Air Transport Auxiliary
BAC	British Aircraft Corporation
BBMF	Battle of Britain Memorial Flight
BMAN	British Marine Air Navigation Co. Ltd
CAACU	Civilian Anti-Aircraft Co-Operation Unit
CAG	Carrier Air Group
CBE	Commander of the British Empire
CFE	Central Fighter Establishment
CO	Commanding Officer
CofG	Centre of Gravity
DFC	Distinguished Flying Cross
DTD	Director of Technical Development
ETPS	Empire Test Pilots School
FAA	Fleet Air Arm
FAI	Federation Aeronautique Internationale
FLS	Fighter Leaders School
FRS	Flying Refresher School
FRU	Fleet Requirements Unit
Gal	General Aircraft
GDC	Group Disbandment Centre
GOR	General Operational Requirement

GSU	Group Support Unit
GWDS	Guided Weapons Development Squadron
HMAS	His Majesty's Australian Ship
HMCS	His Majesty's Canadian Ship
HMS	His/Her Majesty's Ship
IAC	Irish Air Corps
IFTU	Intensive Flying Trials Unit
JAP	J A Prestwich
LAB	Low Altitude Bombing System
MAEE	Maritime Aeroplane Experimental Establishment
MU	Maintenance Unit
NACA	National Advisory Committee for Aeronautics
NATO	North Atlantic Treaty Organisation
NEC	New Engine Company
OCU	Operational Conversion Unit
OTU	Operational Training Unit
PDU	Photographic Development Unit
P&EE	Proof and Experimental Establishment
PG	Photographic Group
PRDU	Photographic Reconnaissance Development Unit
PRU	Photographic Reconnaissance Unit
RAAF	Royal Australian Air Force
RAE	Royal Aircraft Establishment
RATOG	Rocket Assisted Take Off Gear
RCAF	Royal Canadian Air Force
RDAF	Royal Danish Air Force
RN	Royal Navy
RNAS	Royal Naval Air Service/Station
RNAY	Royal Navy Aircraft Yard
RNVR	Royal Naval Volunteer Reserve
RP	Rocket Projectile
SAAF	South African Air Force
SANF	South African Naval Force
SBAC	Society of British Aircraft Constructors
SOC	Struck off Charge
SoTT	School of Technical Training
TAF	Tactical Air Force
THUM	Temperature & Humidity Flight

Supermarine Scimitar F.1 XD215 during carrier trials on HMS *Ark Royal*. (*Aeroplane*)

Aircraft prefix designations

A.D.	Air Development	HF	High-altitude Fighter
ASR	Air-Sea Rescue	LF	Low-altitude Fighter
e	0.5in Browning machine-guns fitted	Mk	Mark
F	Fighter	PR	Photographic Reconnaissance
FAW	Fighter All-Weather	RF	Reconnaissance Fighter
FB	Fighter Bomber	S	Schneider
FR	Fighter Reconnaissance	T	Trainer
		TSR	Tactical Strike and Reconnaissance

The Supermarine Scimitar F.1s of 800 Squadron, led by Lt Cdr D P Norman AFC (in XD231), practising their display routine off the Moray coast, for the 1961 SBAC at Farnborough. (*Aeroplane*)

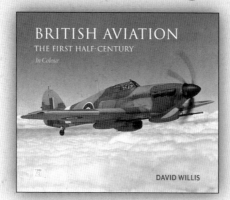